EDUCATION, RELIGION,

AND THE

SUPREME COURT

Edited by

Richard C. McMillan

Published by The Association of Baptist Professors of Religion
P.O. Box 2190   Danville, VA. 24541

To Mary

Printed in the United States of America

for

The Association of Baptist Professors of Religion

P.O. Box 2190   Danville, VA. 24541

ISBN 0-932180-05-1

Library of Congress No. 78-74196

Special Stuides Series No. 6

Cover Logo by Joe Chris Robertson, Mars Hill College

First printed. . . .1979

Table of Contents

Editor's Preface

In 1974 the Association of Baptist Professors of Religion inaugurated the publication of *Perspectives in Religious Studies*, a scholarly journal containing articles and reviews of the widest interest for the professional scholar-teacher. This bold undertaking marked a significant departure for the Association. With only limited funds available it was truly a venture in faith. The journal has been well received and its contribution to the study of religion has been widely acclaimed. It appears three times yearly (Spring, Summer, and Fall).

Early in 1977 the Association began the second phase of its publishing program. This volume marks the sixth offering in the "Special Studies Series." We believe that, together with *Perspectives*, the Special Studies Series will make available the very best scholarly materials to the teacher of religion.

Watson E. Mills
Series Editor

PREFACE

Under the leadership of Thomas Jefferson, James Madison, and others, the framers of the historically unique experiment in representative democracy which brought this Nation into existence added an element to that experimental design calculated to significantly enhance the possibility of success for that design — namely, the Founding Fathers built the separation of religion and government into the Constitution of the United States. The central affirmation of this separation is to be found in the First Amendment to the Constitution which reads in part as follows: "Congress shall make no law respecting an establishment of religion, or prohibiting the free exercise thereof . . ."

Whether 200 or 2000 years old, it is sufficiently difficult to determine the precise meaning of the words used in historic documents; it is often, however, doubly difficult to determine the critically important motivation which stimulated the writing of such documents. Moreover, the meaningful application of historically important documents to the present seems, at times, to baffle even the best of minds. This is no less true of the First Amendment as the continuing so-called "Church-State" debate indicates. While debate over meaning and application is undertaken in the public forum and in scholarly literature, the most significant and determinative focus of debate is to be found in the decisions of the Supreme Court of the United States. In the quarter century just passed, the attempt to apply the First Amendment to contemporary situations resulted in more than fifty major decisions announced by the Court in the area of religion-state relationships.

Based upon the nature of the disputes which generated these decisions, the following categories could be applied to the areas of controversy and litigation: religion and taxation, Sunday observance, religious freedom, ecclesiastical governance, religion and military service (See Appendix B for a listing of the major decisions by the Supreme Court in these areas from 1950-1975.), state aid to parochial education, and religion in public education. While all of these categories are of extreme importance in the continuing debate, state aid to parochial education and the place of religion in public education are of increasing significance and are currently the subject of rather extensive discussion and activity. It is, therefore, the intention of this work to present, in edited form, the major decisions of the Supreme Court of the United States in these two areas of religion-state relationship.

It has been the growing impression of this writer that the decisions of the Supreme Court are among the most discussed but least understood public pronouncements in our society. For example, beginning with *McCollum*, but particularly after *Abington*, it was not at all difficult to hear or read that God had been removed from the public schools. However, many who have read the decisions of the Court are aware that the Court, while ruling against sectarian teaching and devotional exercises, has, nevertheless, left the way clear for more religion, not less, in the possibilities presented by constitutional released time programs (see *Zorach v. Clauson*) and through teaching about religion in the public school setting (see *McCollum v. Board of Education* and *Abington v. Schempp*). Moreover, it is not at all difficult to find expressions of the theme that the state should be able to provide more aid to the financially troubled parochial schools. While direct state aid to such institutions has not been seen as constitutionally permissible, the Court, in *Wolman v. Walter* for example, has demonstrated the legality of more aid, in terms of public welfare legislation, than many persons realize is possible.

At this writing, the debate in these two areas of religion-state concern appears to be intensifying. As the full decisions of the Court are not readily available, it is the intention of the editor to make available, in edited form, the major decisions of the Supreme Court in the two areas of concern in the hope that such information will facilitate our collective efforts toward positive programs and practices which will be in line with the demands of the Constitution.

The decisions of the Court have been edited with the intention to provide the essence of each decision, presenting in this work the major line of reasoning which most clearly develops and clarifies the judgment of the Court. Therefore, the technical legal matters, support data, and elaborative material through which the Court has attempted to develop its position but which is not necessary for understanding a specific decision have been omitted. In short, it has been the goal of the editor to provide the material from the decisions of the Court which will be of most value to those persons who share a concern for either or both of these areas of religion-state controversy, but who have no formal legal training or background. Due to his deep respect for the Court as a vital force in our society and form of government, it is the sincere hope of the editor that no serious damage has been done the decisions by this method of presentation. Aside from an introduction to each chapter, the editor will allow the Court to speak for itself and no comments will be injected into the text of the decisions.

In keeping with the editor's intention in this book, concurring and dissenting opinions, in edited form, are also included with many of the majority decisions of the Court. The concurring opinions are presented when, in the judgment of the editor, such opinions add clarification to the decision of the Court or when they approach the same conclusion as that of the majority from a different and enlightening perspective. The dissenting opinions are included because they present arguments concerning specific constitutional questions which were seriously considered by the Court but, nevertheless, rejected by the majority.

The reader may object to the absence of background material and commentary in this work. While in full sympathy with the need for such material, the editor was prompted to follow the present format by two considerations. First, the pages of historical background, interpretation, and critique written concerning these decisions are extensive and this writer does not feel inspired to add to that material. Given the basic material from the decisions of the Court, the reader is best advised to search out many points of view in his quest for full understanding. Secondly, however, the present writer judged it to be far more important to present, as completely as possible, the material from the decisions themselves inasmuch as this is the most difficult material to obtain. Given this judgment, presentation of adequate background and commentary would have increased the size of this volume well beyond its intended limits.

It must be noted that, in addition to major decisions such as those reproduced in this volume, the Court announces a vast number of brief Memorandum Decisions each term. Despite their importance, it is the judgment of the editor that, in the areas of specific concern reported in this volume, the reader will discover the primary constitutional guidelines in the major decisions of the Court. Therefore, the Memorandum Decisions are not included in this volume.

The arrangement of the book is intended to simplify its use. The first chapter presents the decisions of the Court with respect to the place of religion in public education, and, in the second chapter, the decisions announced in the area of state aid to parochial schools and sectarian institutions of higher education are presented. In order that the reader with specific interests might go directly to the appropriate decision, an introduction is provided for both chapters which briefly summarizes each decision in the chapter.

The reader who desires access to an unedited decision of the Court may turn to one of three sources: the *United States Reports*, published by the United States Government Printing Office; the *Supreme Court Reporter*, published by West Publishing Company; or the *United States Supreme Court Reports, Lawyers' Edition*, published by The Lawyers Co-Operative Publishing Company. Each of these sources has its own citation system for the decisions. As an example, *Wisconsin v. Yoder* may be identified by any one of three citations, depending upon the source: 406 U. S. 205 (the citation system utilized in the *United States Reports*); 32 L. Ed.2d 15 (the citation for the decision in the *Lawyers' Edition*); or 92 S. Ct. 1526 (the citation for the decision as found in the *Supreme Court Reporter*). In all three citation systems, the first number is the volume number; the second number is the page in that volume on which the decision begins. Appendix A provides the three citations for each decision found in this volume.

Every writer or editor owes a formal and public expression of appreciation to many persons. As this editor is no less free of such debt, I want to express my most sincere appreciation to the editor of this monograph series, Dr. Watson E. Mills, of Averett College, for his constant encouragement and invaluable assistance in the completion of this work. I owe a deep expression of gratitude to Dr. W. Waldo Beach, Dr. William H. Cartwright, and, in memorium, to the late Dr. Edward C. Bolmeier, who, during my graduate study at Duke University, greatly stimulated and encouraged my interest in the area of religion-state relationships, particularly with regard to education. And, as in every area of my life, I owe so much to my wife Mary who makes it all worth the effort.

CHAPTER I
RELIGION IN PUBLIC EDUCATION

Introduction

Objection, on religious grounds, to participation in the flag salute ceremony was the occasion for the first decision by the Supreme Court to be presented — the 1940 opinion announced in *Minersville School District v. Gobitis*. With but one Justice dissenting, the Court ruled that a society may utilize its educational system to inculcate those fundamental values to which that society is dedicated and, furthermore, that the requirement of participation in the flag salute ceremony may be a legal and legitimate part of this process of value development.

The *Gobitis* decision was to enjoy a brief life as measured by the normal durability of Supreme Court decisions for only three years later, on June 14, 1943, the Court, in *West Virginia State Board of Education v. Barnette*, overruled that decision. With three Justices dissenting, Mr. Justice Jackson, in presenting the opinion of the Court, undertook the particularly difficult task of reversing a decision of the Court of recent vintage.

According to the analysis of Mr. Justice Jackson, the *Gobitis* decision assumed that the State had the right to impose the flag salute ceremony. The question to which the Court addressed itself in the instant decision, however, asked whether "such a ceremony so touching matters of opinion and political attitude may be imposed upon the individual by official authority ..." (319 U.S., at 636) In answer the Court held that the State has no such authority. The *Gobitis* decision had rested upon an assumption which the Court, in *Barnette*, rejected.

Mr. Justice Frankfurter, who delivered the opinion of the Court in *Gobitis*, wrote a dissenting opinion in *Barnette*. That opinion is reproduced in part. It remained the opinion of Mr. Justice Frankfurter that the Court had, in *Barnette*, infringed seriously upon the legitimate rights of state legislatures to enact laws designed to protect the liberty and welfare of the citizens of that state. Those readers familiar with the broad scope of religion-state litigation will recognize this theme as a recurrent and important one.

The 1948 decision of the Supreme Court in *McCollum v. Board of Education* addressed itself to a form of released time in which religion teachers, sponsored by sectarian groups, were allowed to come into the school buildings of

Champaign County, Illionis, at specified times to provide sectarian instruction to those children whose parents had requested such instruction. According to Mr. Justice Black, the author of the opinion of the Court, such use of tax-supported property for religious education and such a high degree of cooperation between the schools and the religious community were clearly in violation of the First Amendment. Playing a prominent role in the decision was the use of the state's compulsory school attendance laws to enforce attendance in the religion classes.

Mr. Justice Frankfurter also wrote an opinion in the *McCollum* decision; an opinion in which three Justices joined. This opinion, reproduced in part, provides an excellent overview of the religion-state relationship in the history of this Nation and of the development of the released time concept. The result reached in this opinion agreed with the judgment of the Court that the released time plan at bar was unconstitutional, but the opinion also clearly stated that released time, as a broad concept, was not held to violate the Constitution. The Court had ruled here on the released time plan before it, not upon the many variations of this practice which might differ substantially from the one at bar.

A concurring opinion, written by Mr. Justice Jackson, is also reproduced in part as it adds still more important clarification to the position of the Court on this issue. It was Mr. Justice Jackson's notion that it would be impossible, and probably not desirable, to remove all elements of religion from the public schools. His analysis of the place of religion in the public school curriculum in this opinion is one of the more familiar statements in the religion-state controversy to come from the modern Court.

The occasion for *Doremus v. Board of Education* was litigation concerning a New Jersey statute which provided for reading, in the absence of comment, of five verses of the Old Testament at the opening of each public school day. It was the ruling of the Court that no case or controversy existed in this action as presented.

Two important aspects of legal presentation for such an appeal emerged in the analysis of the Court in *Doremus*. First, no offense of constitutional rights was demonstrated to any specific individual or class of individuals. Second, the assertion that tax funds were used in an unconstitutional manner was not demonstrated. In short, it was the sense of the Court that no case or controversy was clearly presented upon whch a ruling could be rendered in terms of the requirements of the First Amendment to the Constitution. This discussion by the Court may, therefore, be viewed as a lesson in the manner in which such issues as might be present should be developed for argument before the Court. Three Justices saw issues in this appeal which should have been argued and dissented from the opinion of the majority.

On March 8, 1948, the Supreme Court announced its decision in *McCollum v. Board of Education*. In that decision, a released time practice was ruled unconstitutional primarily because of the use of tax supported public school facilities for religious instruction. In *Zorach v. Clauson*, announced four years later, a new variation on the released time practice was brought to the Court under the challenge that it, like the practices in *McCollum*, violated the First Amendment to the Constitution.

Mr. Justice Douglas, in delivering the opinion of the Court in *Zorach*, found the challenged New York City plan to be in keeping with "the best of our traditions." (343 U. S., at 314) Under this plan, the schools released students, upon the request of their parents, for religious instruction or activity off the public school property. While the issue of the effect compulsory school attendance laws had on such practices played a prominent role in the *McCollum* decision, the majority saw such laws as of no issue in the instant case. In the view of the majority, either on an occasional basis or as part of an established program, students may be so released from the public schools, leaving public school property and facilities, for religious activity or instruction without violating the First Amendment.

Three Justices dissented from the opinion of the majority and wrote opinions expressing their disagreement. The major issue raised by the dissenting Justices was that of coercion which, in their opinion, operated through compulsory school attendance laws. In their view, one of the basic constitutional flaws of *McCollum* was also very much present in *Zorach*.

Litigation in *Engel v. Vitale* was occasioned by the enactment of legislation in New York which required the opening of each public school day with the recitation of a prayer formulated and recommended by the State Board of Regents. Notwithstanding the fact that participation in the recitation of this prayer was voluntary, the Court, through Mr. Justice Black, expressed the opinion that this practice was clearly one respecting an establishment of religion. Therefore the practice was ruled unconstitutional.

The issue which the Court could not decide in *Doremus* due to technicalities of presentation was, in *Abington v. Schempp*, brought to the Court in justicable form in two companion cases, one from Pennsylvania and a second from Maryland. It was the opinion of the Court that the practice of opening the public school day with required reading from the Bible is a violation of the First Amendment. The list of prior decisions utilized by the majority in this opinion included some of the truly important rulings in religion-state litigation to that point: *Cantwell v. Connecticut*, 310 U. S. 296; *West Virignia Board of Education v. Barnette*, 319 U. S. 624; *Everson v. Board of Education*, 330 U. S. 1; *McCollum v. Board of Education*, 333 U. S. 203; *Zorach v. Clauson*, 343 U. S. 306; *McGowan v. Maryland*, 366 U. S. 420; *Torcaso v. Watkins*, 367 U. S. 488; and *Engel v. Vitale*, 370 U. S. 421.

Mr. Justice Clark, in delivering the opinion of the Court, wrote that any legislation which touches the realm of religion must have "a secular legislative purpose and a primary effect that neither advances nor inhibits religion." (374 U. S., at 222) Legislation must withstand this dual test to survive the restrictions of the Establishment Clause of the First Amendment. In retrospect, this two-pronged test has played a significant role in later rulings by the Court.

Also from the excellent perspective of hindsight, it must be noted that Mr. Justice Clark's statements (374 U. S., at 225) concerning the study of the Bible or religion "when presented objectively as part of a secular program of education" have been formative in the development of approaches to teaching about religion in the public schools.

Concurring opinions were written by Mr. Justice Douglas, Mr. Justice Brennan, and Mr. Justice Goldberg, with whom Mr. Justice Harlan joined. All are reproduced in part as all elaborate and clarify the implications of the Court's decision. The lengthy and complex opinion by Mr. Justice Brennan is especially thorough and would provide valuable insight and information for anyone concerned with the total religion-government relationship. Mr. Justice Stewart's dissenting opinion is also reproduced in part.

In reality, the brief decision in *Chamberlin v. Dade County* is more important for what it did not decide than for what it did decide. Florida statutes requiring Bible reading and prayer in the public schools were held unconstitutional. The other issues — religious and sectarian baccalaureate programs, taking of religious census among children, and the requirement of a religious test for qualification for employment of teachers — were dismissed due to the lack of properly presented federal questions.

Mr. Justice Douglas, Mr. Justice Black, and Mr. Justice Stewart wrote, however, that while there would seem to be no federal question with respect to the baccalaureate services and the religious census, the religious test for teachers should have been argued. It may be that this bit of unfinished business will return in the form of properly presented federal questions — as was the case with *Doremus*.

Arkansas statute provided that to teach the evolutionary theory of Darwin in the public schools and universities of that State constituted a misdemeanor. In *Epperson v. Arkansas*, suit was brought by a teacher who protested that the statute was in violation of her constitutional rights. The Supreme Court ruled that the State may not protect certain religious beliefs or doctrines by prohibiting the teaching in the public schools or universities of theory which might be held to be in violation of those beliefs or doctrines. Such protection is, in effect, an establishment of such beliefs or doctrines.

Concurring opinions were written by Mr. Justice Black, Mr. Justice Harlan, and Mr. Justice Stewart. As the concurring opinions of Mr. Justice Black and Mr. Justice Stewart raise most interesting questions with regard to the ruling, they are reproduced in part.

On June 1, 1925, the Supreme Court, in announcing its decision in *Pierce v. Society of Sisters*, 268 U. S. 510, established the right of parents to choose the type of education their children would enjoy. In that decision, Mr. Justice McReynolds wrote: "The child is not the mere creature of the state; those who nurture him and direct his destiny have the right, coupled with the high duty, to recognize and prepare him for additional obligations." (268 U. S., at 535) Placing great reliance upon the *Pierce* decision along with *Prince v. Massachusetts*, 321 U. S. 158; *Braunfeld v. Brown*, 366 U. S. 599; *Sherbert v. Verner*, 374 U. S. 398; and *Gillette v. United States*, 401 U. S. 437; the Court, in *Wisconsin v. Yoder*, delt with the question of the applicability of Wisconsin's compulsory school attendance laws to children of the Old Order Amish religion. In delivering the opinion of the Court, Mr. Chief Justice Burger argued that the application of compulsory education statutes to children of this faith beyond elementary school would be in violation of the guarantees of the First Amendment.

The critical element in the decision was the religious rights under consideration. "A way of life, however virtuous and admirable, may not be interposed as a barrier to reasonable state regulation of education if it is based on purely secular considerations; to have the protection of the Religion Clause, the claims must be rooted in religious belief." (406 U. S., at 215) As *Pierce* gave legal status to the parent's choice to send his child to some form of formal schooling, meeting state standards, other than the public school, *Yoder* extended this legal status to certain forms of informal schooling, but only in terms of very specific conditions — namely, the experience of basic formal education by the children in question and clear evidence that formal education beyond that point would violate deeply held religious beliefs. Great care was taken by the Court to limit the application of this decision to a very restricted set of circumstances.

MINERSVILLE SCHOOL DIST v. GOBITIS.

310 U. S. 586

Decided June 3, 1940 — one Justice dissenting.

Mr. Justice FRANKFURTER delivered the opinion of the Court.

A grave responsibility confronts this Court whenever in course of litigation it must reconcile the conflicting claims of liberty and authority. But when the liberty invoked is liberty of conscience, and the authority is authority to safeguard the nation's fellowship, judicial conscience is put to its severest test. Of such a nature is the present controversy.

Lillian Gobitis, aged twelve, and her brother William, aged ten, were expelled from the public schools of Minersville, Pennsylvania, for refusing to salute the national flag as part of a daily school exercise. The local Board of Education required both teachers and pupils to participate in this ceremony.... The Gobitis family are affiliated with "Jehovah's Witnesses", for whom the Bible as the Word of God is the supreme authority. The children had been brought up conscientiously to believe that such a gesture of respect for the flag was forbidden by command of scripture.

The Gobitis children were of an age for which Pennsylvania makes school attendance compulsory. Thus they were denied a free education and their parents had to put them into private schools. To be relieved of the financial burden thereby entailed, their father, on behalf of the children and in his own behalf, brought this suit.

We must decide whether the requirement of participation in such a ceremony, exacted from a child who refuses upon sincere religious grounds, infringes without due process of law the liberty guaranteed by the Fourteenth Amendment.

Centuries of strife over the erection of particular dogmas as exclusive or all-comprehending faiths led to the inclusion of a guarantee for religious freedom in the Bill of Rights. The First Amendment, and the Fourteenth through its absorption of the First, sought to guard against repetition of those bitter religious struggles by prohibiting the establishment of a state religion and by securing to every sect the free exercise of its faith.

Certainly the affirmative pursuit of one's convictions about the ultimate mystery of the universe and man's relation to it is placed beyond the reach of law. Government may not interfere with organized or individual expression of belief or disbelief. Propagation of belief — or even of disbelief in the supernatural — is protected, whether in church or chapel, mosque or synagogue, tabernacle or meetinghouse. Likewise the Constitution assures generous immunity to the individual from imposition of penalties for offending, in the course of his own religious activities, the religious views of others, be they a minority or those who are dominant in government.

When does the constitutional guarantee compel exemption from doing what society thinks necessary for the promotion of some great common end, or from a penalty for conduct which appears dangerous to the general good? To state the problem is to recall the truth that no single principle can answer all of life's complexities. The right to freedom of religious belief, however dissident and however obnoxious to the cherished beliefs of others — even of a majority — is itself the denial of an absolute. But to affirm that the freedom to follow conscience has itself no limits in the life of a society would deny that very plurality of principles which, as a matter of history, underlies protection of religious toleration.... Our present task then, as so often the case with courts, is to reconcile two rights in order to prevent either from destroying the other.

Conscientious scruples have not, in the course of the long struggle for religious toleration, relieved the individual from obedience to a general law not aimed at the promotion or restriction of religious beliefs. The mere possession of religious convictions which contradict the relevant concerns of a political society does not relieve the citizen from the discharge of political responsibilities. The necessity for this adjustment has again and again been recognized.

The ultimate foundation of a free society is the binding tie of cohesive sentiment. Such a sentiment is fostered by all those agencies of the mind and spirit which may serve to gather up the traditions of a people, transmit them from generation to generation, and thereby create that continuity of a treasured common life which constitutes a civilization.

The precise issue, then, for us to decide is wether the legislatures of the various states and the authorities in a thousand counties and school districts of this country are barred from determining the appropriateness of various means to evoke that unifying sentiment without which there can ultimately be no liberties, civil or religious.

What the school authorities are really asserting is the right to awaken in the child's mind considerations as to the significance of the flag contrary to those implanted by the parent. In such an attempt the state is normally at a disadvantage in competing with the parent's authority, so long — and this is the vital aspect of religious toleration — as parents are unmolested in their right to counteract by their own persuasiveness the wisdom and rightness of those loyalties which the state's educational system is seeking to promote.... That the flag-salute is an allowable portion of a school program for those who do not invoke conscientious scruples is surely not debatable. But for us to insist that, though the ceremony may be required, exceptional immunity must be given to dissidents, is to maintain that there is no basis for a legislative judgment that such an exemption might introduce elements of difficulty into the school discipline, might cast doubts in the minds of the other children which would themselves weaken the effect of the exercise.

The preciousness of the family relation, the authority and independence which give dignity to parenthood, indeed the enjoyment of all freedom, presuppose the kind of ordered society which is summarized by our flag. A society which is dedicated to the preservation of these ultimate values of civilization may in self-protection utilize the educational process for inculcating those almost unconscious feelings which bind men together in a comprehending loyalty, whatever may be their lesser differences and difficulties.

Mr. Justice STONE (dissenting).

. . . by this law the state seeks to coerce these children to express a sentiment which, as they interpret it, they do not entertain, and which violates their deepest religious convictions. It is not denied that such compulsion is a prohibited infringement of personal liberty, freedom of speech and religion, guaranteed by the Bill of Rights, except in so far as it may be justified and supported as a proper exercise of the state's power over public education.

Concededly the constitutional guarantees of personal liberty are not always absolutes. . . . But it is a long step, and one which I am unable to take, to the position that government may, as a supposed educational measure and as a means of disciplining the young, compel public affirmations which violate their religious conscience.

. . . even if we believe that such compulsions will contribute to national unity, there are other ways to teach loyalty and patriotism which are the sources of national unity, than by compelling the pupil to affirm that which he does not believe and by commanding a form of affirmance which violates his religious convictions. Without recourse to such compulsion the state is free to compel attendance at school and require teaching by instruction and study of all in our history and in the structure and organization of our government, including the guarantees of civil liberty which tend to inspire patriotism and love of country.

The Constitution may well elicit expressions of loyalty to it and to the government which it created, but it does not command such expressions or otherwise give any indication that compulsory expressions of loyalty play any such part in our scheme of government as to override the constitutional protection of freedom of speech and religion.

The Constitution expresses more than the conviction of the people that democratic processes must be preserved at all costs. It is also an expression of faith and a command that freedom of mind and spirit must be preserved, which government must obey, if it is to adhere to that justice and moderation without which no free government can exist.

WEST VIRGINIA STATE BOARD OF EDUCATION v. BARNETTE.

319 U. S. 624

Decided June 14, 1943 — three Justices dissenting.

Mr. Justice JACKSON delivered the opinion of the Court.

Following the decision by this Court on June 3, 1940, in *Minersville School District v. Gobitis*, 310 U. S. 586, 1943, the West Virignia legislature amended its statutes to require all schools therein to conduct courses of instruction in history, civics, and in the Constitutions of the United States and of the State "for the purpose of teaching, fostering and perpetuating the ideals, principles and spirit of Americanism, and increasing the knowledge of the organization and machinery of the government."

The Board of Education on January 9, 1942, adopted a resolution containing recitals taken largely from the Court's *Gobitis* opinion and ordering that the salute to the flag become "a regular part of the program of activities in the public schools," that all teachers and pupils "shall be required to participate in the salute honoring the Nation represented by the Flag; provided, however, that refusal to salute the Flag be regarded as an Act of insubordination, and shall be dealt with accordingly."

Failure to conform is "insubordination" dealt with by expulsion. Readmission is denied by statute until compliance. Meanwhile the expelled child is "unlawfully absent" and may be proceeded against as a delinquent. His parents or guardians are liable to prosecution . . .

Appellees, citizens of the United States and of West Virginia, brought suit in the United States District Court for themselves and others similarly situated asking its injunction to restrain enforcement of these laws and regulations against Jehovah's Witnesses. The Witnesses are an unincorporated body teaching that the obligation imposed by law of God is superior to that of laws enacted by temporal government.

Children of this faith have been expelled from school and are threatened with exclusion for no other cause. Officials threaten to send them to reformatories maintained for criminally inclined juveniles. Parents of such children have been prosecuted and are threatened with prosecutions for causing delinquency.

This case calls upon us to reconsider a precedent decision, as the Court throughout its history often has been required to do. Before turning to the *Gobitis* case, however, it is desirable to notice certain characteristics by which this controversy is distinguished.

. . . the refusal of these persons to participate in the ceremony does not interfere with or deny rights of others to do so. Nor is there any question in this case that their behavior is peaceable and orderly. The sole conflict is between authority and rights of the individual. The State asserts power to condition access to public education on making a prescribed sign and profession and at the same time to coerce attendance by punishing both parent and child. The latter stand on a right of self-determination in matters that touch individual opinion and personal attitude.

As the present Chief Justice said in dissent in the *Gobitis* case, the State may "require teaching by instruction and study of all in our history and in the structure and organization of our government . . ." Here, however, we are dealing with a compulsion of students to declare a belief. . . . The issue here is whether this slow and easily neglected route to aroused loyalties constitutionally may be short-cut by substituting a compulsory salute and slogan.

Symbols of State often convey political ideas just as religious symbols come to convey theological ones. Associated with many of these symbols are appropriate gestures of acceptance or respect: a salute, a bowed or bared head, a bended knee. A person gets from a symbol the meaning he puts into it, and what is one man's comfort and inspiration is another's jest and scorn.

. . . here the power of compulsion is invoked without any allegation that remaining passive during a flag salute ritual creates a clear and present danger that would justify an effort even to muffle expression. To sustain the compulsory flag salute we are required to say that a Bill of Rights which guards the individual's right to speak his own mind, left it open to public authorities to compel him to utter what is not in his mind.

. . . validity of the asserted power to force an American citizen publicly to profess any statement of belief or to engage in any ceremony of assent to one presents questions of power that must be considered independently of any idea we may have as to the utility of the ceremony in question.

While religion supplies appellees' motive for enduring the discomforts of making the issue in this case, many citizens who do not share these religious views hold a compulsory rite to infringe constitutional liberty of the individual. It is not necessary to inquire whether non-conformist beliefs will exempt from the duty to salute unless we first find power to make the salute a legal duty.

The *Gobitis* decision, however, *assumed*, as did the argument in that case and in this, that power exists in the State to impose the flag salute discipline upon school children in general. The Court only examined and rejected a claim based on religious beliefs of immunity from an unquestioned general rule. The question which underlies the flag salute controversy is whether such a ceremony so touching matters of opinion and political attitude may be imposed upon the individual by official authority under powers committed to any political organization under our Constitution.

Government of limited power need not be anemic government. Assurance that rights are secure tends to diminish fear and jealousy of strong government, and by making us feel safe to live under it makes for its better support.

Free public education, if faithful to the ideal of secular instruction and political neutrality, will not be partisan or enemy of any class, creed, party, or faction. If it is to impose any ideological discipline, however, each party or denomination must seek to control, or failing that, to weaken the influence of the educational system. Observance of the limitations of the Constitution will not weaken government in the field appropriate for its exercise.

The Fourteenth Amendment, as now applied to the States, protects the citizen against the State itself and all of its creatures — Boards of Education not excepted. These have, of course, important, delicate, and highly discretionary functions, but none that they may not perform within the limits of the Bill of Rights. That they are educating the young for citizenship is reason for scrupulous protection of Constitutional freedoms of the individual, if we are not to strangle the free mind at its source and teach youth to discount important principles of our government as mere platitudes.

The action of Congress in making flag observance voluntary and respecting the conscinece of the objector in a matter so vital as raising the Army contrasts sharply with these local regulations in matters relatively trivial to the welfare of the nation.

The very purpose of a Bill of Rights was to withdraw certain subjects from the vicissitudes of political controversy, to place them beyond the reach of majorities and officials and to establish them as legal principles to be appled by the Courts. One's right to life, liberty, and property, to free speech, a free press, freedom of worship and assembly, and other fundamental rights may not be submitted to vote; they depend on the outcome of no elections.

. . . the task of translating the majestic generalities of the Bill of Rights, conceived as part of the pattern of liberal government in the eighteenth century, into concrete restraints on officials dealing with the problems of the twentieth century, is one to disturb self-confidence. These principles grew in soil which also produced a philosophy that the individual was the center of society, that his liberty was attainable through mere absence of governmental restraints, and that government should be entrusted with few controls and only the mildest supervision over man's affairs. We must transplant these rights to a soil in which the *laissez-faire* concept or principle of non-interference has withered at least as to economic affairs, and social advancements are increasingly sought through closer integration of society and through expanded and strengthened governmental controls. These changed conditions often deprive precedents of reliability and cast us more than we would choose upon our own judgment. But we act in these matters not by authority of our competence but by force of our commissions. We cannot, because of modest estimates of our competence in such specialities as public education, withhold the judgment that history authenticates as the function of this Court when liberty is infringed.

Struggles to coerce uniformity of sentiment in support of some end thought essential to their time and country have been waged by many good as well as evil men. . . . Those who begin coercive elimination of dissent soon find themselves exterminating dissenters. Compulsory unification of opinion achieves only the unanimity of the graveyard.

It seems trite but necessary to say that the First Amendment to our Constitution was designed to avoid these ends by avoiding these beginnings. There is no mysticism in the American concept of the State or of the nature or origin of its authority. We set up government by consent of the governed, and the Bill of Rights denies those in power any legal opportunity to coerce that consent. Authority here is to be controlled by public opinion, not public opinion by authority.

The case is made difficult not because the principles of its decision are obscure but because the flag involved is our own. Nevertheless, we apply the limitations of the Constitution with no fear that freedom to be intellectually and spiritually diverse or even contrary will disintegrate the social organization. To believe that patriotism will not flourish if patriotic ceremonies are voluntary and spontaneous instead of a compulsory routine is to make an unflattering estimate of the appeal of our institutions to free minds. . . . freedom to differ is not limited to things that do not matter much. That would be a mere shadow of freedom. The test of its substance is the right to differ as to things that touch the heart of the existing order.

If there is any fixed star in our constitutional constellation, it is that no official, high or petty, can prescribe what shall be orthodox in politics, nationalism, religion, or other matters of opinion or force citizens to confess by word or act their faith therein. If there are any circumstances which permit an exception, they do not now occur to us.

We think the action of the local authorities in compelling the flag salute and pledge transcends constitutional limitations on their power and invades the sphere of intellect and spirit which it is the purpose of the First Amendment to our Constitution to reserve from all official control.

The decision of this Court in *Minersville School District v. Gobitis* and the holdings of those few per curiam decisions which preceded and foreshadowed it are overrulled, and the judgment enjoining enforcement of the West Virginia Regulation is affirmed.

Mr. Justice BLACK and Mr. Justice DOUGLAS, concurring.

We are substantially in agreement with the opinion just read, but since we originally joined with the Court in the *Gobitis* case, it is appropriate that we make a brief statement of reasons for our change of view.

Reluctance to make the Federal Constitution a rigid bar against state regulation of conduct thought inimical to the public welfare was the controlling influence which moved us to consent to the *Gobitis* decision. Long reflection convinced us that although the principle is sound, its application in the particular case was wrong.

No well-ordered society can leave to the individuals an absolute right to make final decisions, unassilable by the State, as to everything they will or will not do. The First Amendment does not go so far. Religious faiths, honestly held, do not free individuals from responsibility to conduct themselves obediently to laws which are either imperatively necessary to protect society as a whole from grave and pressingly imminent dangers or which, without any general prohibition, merely regulate time, place or manner of religious activity.

Words uttered under coercion are proof of loyalty to nothing but self-interest. Love of country must spring from willing hearts and free minds, inspired by a fair administration of wise laws enacted by the people's elected representatives within the bounds of express constitutional prohibitions.

Neither our domestic tranquility in peace nor our martial effort in war depend on compelling little children to participate in a ceremony which ends in nothing for them but a fear of spiritual condemnation.

Mr. Justice FRANKFURTER, dissenting.

As a member of this Court I am not justified in writing my private notions of policy into the Constitution, no matter how deeply I may cherish them or how mischievous I may deem their disregard. The duty of a judge who must decide which of two claims before the Court shall prevail, that of a State to enact and enforce laws within its general competence or that of an individual to refuse obedience because of the demands of his conscience, is not that of the ordinary person. It can never be emphasized too much that one's own opinion about the wisdom or evil of a law should be excluded altogether when one is doing one's duty on the bench. The only opinion of our own even looking in that direction that is material is our opinion whether legislators could in reason have enacted such a law. In the light of all the circumstances, including the history of this question in this Court, it would require more daring that I possess to deny that reasonable legislators could have taken the action which is before us for review. Most unwillingly, therefore, I must differ from my brethren with regard to legislation like this.

When Mr. Justice Holmes, speaking for this Court, wrote that "it must be remembered that legislatures are ultimate guardians of the liberties and welfare of the people in quite as great a degree as the courts". . . he went to the very essence of our constitutional system and the democratic conception of our society. . . . responsibility for legislation lies with legislatures, answerable as they are directly to the people, and this Court's only and very narrow function is to determine whether within the broad grant of authority vested in legislatures they have exercised a judgment for which reasonable justification can be offered.

We are not reviewing merely the action of a local school baord. The flag salute requirement in this case comes before us with the full authority of the State of West Virginia. We are in fact passing judgment on "the power of the State as a whole". . . . Practically we are passing upon the political power of each of the forty-eight states. Moreover, since the First Amendment has been read into the Fourteenth, our problem is precisely the same as it would be if we had before us an Act of Congress for the District of Columbia. To suggest that we are here concerned with the heedless action of some village tyrants is to distort the augustness of the constitutional issue and the reach of the consequences of our decision.

Under our constitutional system the legislature is charged solely with civil concerns of society. If the avowed or intrinsic legislative purpose is either to promote or to discourage some religious community or creed, it is clearly within the constitutional restrictions imposed on legislatures and cannot stand. But it by no means follows that legislative power is wanting whenever a general non-discriminatory civil regulation in fact touches conscientious scruples or religious beliefs of an individual or a group.

A court can only strike down. It can only say "This or that law is void." It cannot modify or qualify, it cannot make exceptions to a general requirement. And it strikes down not merely for a day. At least the finding of unconstitutionality ought not to have ephemeral significance unless the Constitution is to be reduced to the fugitive importance of mere legislation.

What one can say with assurance is that the history out of which grew constitutional provisions for religious equality and the writings of the great exponents of religious freedom — Jefferson, Madison, John Adams, Benjamin Franklin — are totally wanting in justification for a claim by dissidents of exceptional immunity from civic measures of general applicability, measures not in fact disguised assaults upon such dissident views.

The constitutional protection of religious freedom terminated disabilities, it did not create new privileges. It gave religious equality, not civil immunity. Its essence is freedom from conformity to religious dogma, not freedom from conformity to law because of religious dogma.

Any person may . . . believe or disbelieve what he pleases. He may practice what he will in his own house of worship or publicly within the limits of public order. But the lawmaking authority is not circumscribed by the variety of religious beliefs, otherwise the constitutional guaranty would be not a protection of the free exercise of religion but a denial of the exercise of legislation.

The essence of the religious freedom guaranteed by our Constitution is therefore this: no religion shall either receive the state's support or incur its hostility. Religion is outside the sphere of political government. This does not mean that all matters on which religious organizations or beliefs may pronounce are outside the sphere of government. Were this so, instead of the separation of church and state, there would be the subordination of the state on any matter deemed within the soverignty of the religious conscience.

An act compelling profession of allegiance to a religion, no matter how subtly or tenuously promoted, is bad. But an act promoting good citizenship and national allegiance is within the domain of governmental authority and is therefore to be judged by the same considerations of power and of constitutionality as those involved in the many claims of immunity from civil obedience because of religious scruples.

Law is concerned with external behavior and not with the inner life of man. . . . The individual conscience may profess what faith it chooses. It may affirm and promote that faith . . . but it cannot thereby restrict community action through political organs in matters of community concern, so long as the action is not asserted in a discriminatory way either openly or by stealth. One may have the right to practice one's religion and at the same time owe the duty of formal obedience to laws that run counter to one's beliefs.

That which to the majority may seem essential for the welfare of the state may offend the consciences of a minority. But, so long as no inroads are made upon the actual exercise of religion by the minority, to deny the political power of the majority to enact laws concerned with civil matters, simply because they may offend the consciences of a minority, really means that the consciences of a minority are more sacred and more enshrined in the Constitution than the consciences of a majority.

*PEOPLE OF STATE OF ILLINOIS ex rel.
McCOLLUM v. BOARD OF EDUCATION OF
SCHOOL DIST. NO. 71, CHAMPAIGN COUNTY,
ILL.*

333 U. S. 203

Decided March 8, 1948 — one Justice dissenting.

Mr. Justice BLACK delivered the opinion of the Court.

This case relates to the power of a state to utilize its tax-supported public school system in aid of religious instruction insofar as that power may be restricted by the First and Fourteenth Amendments to the Federal Constitution.

Appellant's petition for mandamus alleged that religious teachers, employed by private religious groups, were permitted to come weekly into the school buildings during the regular hours set apart for secular teaching, and then and there for a period of thirty minutes substitute their religious teaching for the secular education provided under the compulsory education law. The petitioner charged that this joint public-school religious-group program violated the First and Fourteenth Amendments to the United States Constitution.

Although there are disputes between the parties as to various inferences that may or may not properly be drawn from the evidence concerning the religious program, the following facts are shown by the record without dispute. In 1940 interested members of the Jewish, Roman Catholic, and a few of the Protestant faiths formed a voluntary association called the Champaign Council on Religious Education. They obtained permission from the Board of Education to offer classes in religious instruction to public school pupils in grades four to nine inclusive. Classes were made up of pupils whose parents signed printed cards requesting that their children be permitted to attend; they were held weekly, thirty minutes for the lower grades, forty-five minutes for the higher. The council employed the religious teachers at no expense to the school authorities, but the instructors were subject to the approval and supervision of the superintendent of schools. The classes were taught in three separate religious groups by Protestant teachers, Catholic priests, and a Jewish rabbi . . . Classes were conducted in the regular classrooms of the school building. Students who did not choose to take the religious instruction were not released from public school duties; they were required to leave their classrooms and go to some other place in the school building for pursuit of their secular studies. On the other hand, students who were released from secular study for the religious instructions were required to be present at the religious classes. Reports of their presence or absence were to be made to their secular teachers.

The foregoing facts, without reference to others that appear in the record, show the use of tax-supported property for religious instruction and the close cooperation between the school authorities and the religious council in promoting religious education. The operation of the state's compulsory education system thus assists and is integrated with the program of religious instruction carried on by separate religious sects. Pupils compelled by law to go to school for secular education are released in part from their legal duty upon the condition that they attend the religious classes. This is beyond all question a utilization of the tax-established and tax-supported public school system to aid religious groups to spread their faith. And it falls squarely under the ban of the First Amendment . . .

To hold that a state cannot consistently with the First and Fourteenth Amendments utilize its public school system to aid any or all religious faiths or sects in the dissemination of their doctrines and ideals does not, as counsel urge, manifest a governmental hostility to religion or religious teachings. A manifestation of such hostility would be at war with our national tradition as embodied in the First Amendment's guaranty of the free exercise of religion. For the First Amendment rests upon the premise that both religion and government can best work to achieve their lofty aims if each is left free from the other within its respective sphere.

Here not only are the state's tax-supported public school buildings used for the dissemination of religious doctrines. The State also affords sectarian groups an invaluable aid in that it helps to provide pupils for their religious classes through use of the state's compulsory public school machinery. This is not separation of Church and State.

Mr. Justice FRANKFURTER delivered the following opinion in which Mr. Justice JACKSON, Mr. Justice RUTLEDGE and Mr. Justice BURTON join.

We dissented in *Everson v. Board of Education*, 330 U. S. 1, because in our view the Constitutional principle requiring separation of Church and State compelled invalidation of the ordinance sustained by the majority. Illinois has here authorized the commingling of sectarian with secular instruction in the public schools. The Constitution of the United States forbids this.

The case, in the light of the *Everson* decision, demonstrates anew that the mere formulation of a relevant Constitutional principle is the beginning of the solution of a problem, not its answer. . . . We are all agreed that the First and the Fourteenth Amendments have a secular reach far more penetrating in the conduct of Government than merely to forbid an "established church." But agreement, in the abstract, that the First Amendment was designed to erect a "wall of separation between Church and State," does not preclude a clash of views as to what the wall separates.

To understand the particular program now before us as a conscientious attempt to accommodate the allowable functions of Government and the special concerns of the Church within the framework of our Constitution and with due regard to the kind of society for which it was designed, we must put this Champaign program of 1940 in its historic setting. Traditionally, organized education in the Western world was Church education.

The emigrants who came to these shores brought this view of education with them. Colonial schools certainly started with a religious orientation.

The evolution of colonial education, largely in the service of religion, into the public school system of today is the story of changing conceptions regarding the

American democratic society, of the functions of State-maintained education in such a society, and of the role therein of the free exercise of religion by the people. The modern public school derived from a philosophy of freedom reflected in the First Amendment. . . . As the momentum for popular education increased and in turn evoked strong claims for State support of religious education, contests not unlike that which in Virginia had produced Madison's Remonstrance appeared in various form in other States. New York and Massachusetts provided famous chapters in the history that established dissociation of religious teaching from State-maintained schools. . . . The upshot of these controversies, often long and fierce, is fairly summarized by saying that long before the Fourteenth Amendment subjected the States to new limitations, the prohibition of furtherance by the State of religious instruction became the guiding principle, in law and feeling, of the American people.

It is pertinent to remind that the establishment of this principle of separtion in the field of education was not due to any decline in the religious beliefs of the people. Horace Mann was a devout Christian, and the deep religious feeling of James Madison is stamped upon the Remonstrance. The secular public school did not imply indifference to the basic role of religion in the life of the people, nor rejection of religious education as a means of fostering it. . . . The sharp confinement of the public schools to secular education was a recognition of the need of a democratic society to educate its children, insofar as the State undertook to do so, in an atmosphere free from pressures in a realm in which pressures are most resisted and where conflicts are most easily and most bitterly engendered. Designed to serve as perhaps the most powerful agency for promoting cohesion among a heterogeneous democratic people, the public school must keep scrupulously free from entanglement in the strife of sects. The preservation of the community from divisive conflicts, of Government from irreconcilable pressures by religious groups, of religion from censorship and coercion however subtly exercised, requires strict confinement of the State to instruction other than religious, leaving to the individual's church and home, indoctrination in the faith of his choice.

Prohibition of the commingling of sectarian and secular instruction in the public school is of course only half the story. A religious people was naturally concerned about the part of the child's education entrusted "to the family altar, the church, and the private school." The promotion of religious education took many forms. Laboring under financial difficulties and exercising only persuasive authority, various denominations felt handicapped in their task of religious education. . . . But the major efforts of religious inculcation were a recognition of the principle of Separation by the establishment of church schools privately supported. Parochial schools were maintained by various denominations. . . . There were experiments with vacation schools, with Saturday as well as Sunday schools. They all fell short of their purpose.

Out of these inadequate efforts evolved the week-day church school, held on one or more afternoons a week after the close of the public school. But children continued to be children . . . Church leaders decided that if the week-day church school was to succeed, a way had to be found to give the child his religious education during what the child conceived to be his "business hours."

The initiation of the movement may fairly be attributed to Dr. George U. Wenner. The underlying assumption of his proposal, made at the Interfaith Conference on

Federation held in New York City in 1905, was that the public school unduly monopolized the child's time and that the churches were entitled to their share of it. This, the schools should "release." Accordingly, the Federation, citing the example of the Third Republic of France, urged that upon the request of their parents children be excused from public school on Wednesday afternoon, so that the churches could provide "Sunday school on Wednesday."

The proposal aroused considerable opposition and it took another decade for a "released time" scheme to become part of a public school system. Gary, Indiana, inaugurated the movement. . . . [Superintendent of Schools] Wirt's plan sought to rotate the schedules of the children during the school-day so that some were in class, others were in the library, still others on the playground. And some, he suggested to the leading ministers of the City, might be released to attend religious classes if the churches of the City cooperated and provided them. They did, in 1914, and thus was "released time" begun. The religious teaching was held on church premises and the public schools had no hand in the conduct of these church schools.

From such a beginning "released time" has attained substantial proportions.

Of course, "released time" as a generalized conception, undefined by differentiating particularities, is not an issue for Constitutional adjudication. Local programs differ from each other in many and crucial respects. . . . It is only when challenge is made to the share that the public schools have in the execution of a particular "released time" program that close judicial scrutiny is demanded of the exact relation between the religious instruction and the public educational system in the specific situation before the Court.

Religious education . . . conducted on school time and property is patently woven into the working scheme of the school. The Champaign arrangement thus presents powerful elements of inherent pressure by the school system in the interest of religious sects. . . . Separation is a requirement to abstain from fusing functions of Government and of religious sects, not merely to treat them all equally. That a child is offered an alternative may reduce the constraint; it does not eliminate the operation of influence by the school in matters sacred to conscience and outside the school's domain. The law of imitation operates, and nonconformity is not an outstanding characteristic of children. The result is an obvious pressure upon children to attend. Again, while the Champaign school population represents only a fraction of the more than two hundred and fifty sects of the nation, not even all the practicing sects in Champaign are willing or able to provide religious instruction. . . . As a result, the public school system of Champaign actively furthers inculcation in the religious tenets of some faiths, and in the process sharpens the consciousness of religious differences at least among some of the children committed to its care.

We do not consider, as indeed we could not, school programs not before us which, though colloquially characterized as "released time," present situations differing in aspects that may well be constitutionally crucial.

Separation means separation, not something less. Jefferson's metaphor in describing the relation between Chruch and State speaks of a "wall of separation," not of a fine line easily overstepped. The public school is at once the symbol of our democracy and the most pervasive means for promoting our common destiny. In no activity of the State is it more vital to keep out divisive forces than in its schools, to avoid confusing, not to say fusing, what the

Constitution sought to keep strictly apart.

Mr. Justice JACKSON, concurring.

I join the opinion of Mr. Justice FRANKFURTER, and concur in the result reached by the Court, but with these reservations: I think it is doubtful whether the facts of this case establish jurisdiction in this Court, but in any event that we should place some bounds on the demands for interference with local schools that we are empowered or willing to entertain.

A Federal Court may interfere with local school authorities only when they invade either a personal liberty or a property right protected by the Federal Constitution. Ordinarily this will come about in either of two ways:

First. When a person is required to submit to some religious rite or instruction or is deprived or threatened with deprivation of his freedom for resisting such unconstitutional requirement.

Second. Where a complainant is deprived of property by being taxed for unconstitutional purposes, such as directly or indirectly to support a religious establishment.

If . . . jurisdiction is found to exist, it is important that we circumscribe our decision with some care. . . . The plaintiff, as she has every right to be, is an avowed atheist. What she has asked of the courts is that they not only end the "released time" plan but also ban every form of teaching which suggests or recognizes that there is a God. . . . This Court is directing the Illinois courts generally to sustain plaintiff's complaint without exception of any of these grounds of complaint, without discriminating between them and without laying down any standards to define the limits of the effect of our decision.

To me, the sweep and detail of these complaints is a danger signal which warns of the kind of local controversy we will be required to arbitrate if we do not place appropriate limitation on our decision and exact strict compliance with jurisdictional requirements.

While we may and should end such formal and explicit instruction as the Champaign plan and can at all times prohibit teaching of creed and catechism and ceremonial and can forbid forthright proselyting in the schools, I think it remains to be demonstrated whether it is possible, even if desirable, to comply with such demands as plaintiff's completely to isolate and cast out of secular education all that some people may reasonably regard as religious instruction. Perhaps subjects such as mathematics, physics or chemistry are, or can be, completely secularized. But it would not seem practical to teach either practice or appreciation of the arts if we are to forbid exposure of youth to any religious influences. Music without sacred music, architecture minus the cathedral, or painting without the scriptural themes would be eccentric and incomplete, even from a secular point of view. Yet the inspirational appeal of religion in these guises is often stronger than in forthright sermon. Even such a "science" as biology raises the issue between evolution and creation as an explanation of our presence on this planet. Certainly a course in English literature that omitted the Bible and other powerful uses of our mother tongue for religious ends would be pretty barren. And I should suppose it is a proper, if not an indispensable, part of preparation for a worldly life to know the roles that religion and religions have played in the tragic story of mankind. The fact is that, for good or for ill, nearly everything in our culture worth transmitting, everything which gives meaning to life, is saturated with religious influences, derived from paganism, Judaism, Christianity — both Catholic and Protestant — and other faiths accepted by a large part of the world's peoples. One can hardly respect a system of education that would leave the student wholly ignorant of the currents of religious thought that move the world society for a part in which he is being prepared.

But how one can teach, with satisfaction or even with justice to all faiths, such subjects as the story of the Reformation, the Inquisition, or even the New England effort to found "a Church without a Bishop and a State without a King," is more than I know. It is too much to expect that mortals will teach subjects about which their contemporaries have passonate controversies with the detachment they may summon to teaching about remote subjects such as Confucius or Mohamet.

The opinions in this case show that public educational authorities have evolved a considerable variety of practices in dealing with the religious problem. Neighborhoods differ in racial, religious and cultural compositions. . . . We must leave some flexibility to meet local conditions, some chance to progress by trial and error. While I agree that the religious classes involved here go beyond permissible limits, I also think the complaint demands more than plaintiff is entitled to have granted. So far as I can see this Court does not tell the State court where it may stop, nor does it set up any standards by which the State court may determine that question for itself.

DOREMUS v. BOARD OF EDUCATION OF BOROUGH OF HAWTHORNE.

342 U. S. 429

Decided March 3, 1952 — three Justices dissenting.

Mr. Justice JACKSON delivered the opinion of the Court.

This action for a declaratory judgment on a question of federal constitutional law was prosecuted in the state courts of New Jersey. It sought to declare invalid a statute of that State which provides for the reading, without comment, of five verses of the Old Testament at the opening of each public-school day. . . . No issue was raised under the State Constitution, but the Act was claimed to violate the clause of the First Amendment to the Federal Constitution prohibiting establishment of religion.

No trial was held and we have no findings of fact, but the trial court denied relief on the merits on the basis of the pleadings and a pretrial conference, of which the record contains meager notes. The Supreme Court of New Jersey, on appeal, rendered its opinion that the Act does not violate the Federal Constitution, in spite of jurisdictional doubts which it pointed out but condoned as follows: "No one is before us asserting that his religious practices have been interfered with or that his right to worship in accordance with the dictates of his conscience has been suppressed. No religious sect is a party to the cause. No representative of, or spokesman for, a religious body has attacked the statute here or below. One of the plaintiffs is 'a citizen and taxpayer'; the only interest he asserts is just that . . . The other plaintiff, in addition to being a citizen and a taxpayer, has a daughter, aged seventeen, who is a student of the school. Those facts are asserted, but, as in the case of the co-plaintiff, no violated rights are urged. It is not charged that the practice required by the statute conflicts with the convictions of either mother or daughter. Apparently the sole purpose and the only function of plaintiffs is that they shall assume the role of actors so that there may be a suit which will invoke a court ruling upon the constitutionality of the statute. . . ."

The view of the facts taken by the court below, though it is entitled to respect, does not bind us and we may make an independent examination of the record. Doing so, we find nothing more substantial in support of jurisdiction than did the court below. Appellants, apparently seeking to bring themselves within *Illinois ex rel. McCollum v. Board of Education of School Dist. No. 71*, 333 U. S. 203, assert a challenge to the Act in two capacities — one as parent of a child subject to it, and both as taxpayers burdened because of its requirements.

In support of the parent-and-school-child relationship, the complaint alleged that appellant Klein was parent of a seventeen-year-old pupil in Hawthorne High School, where Bible reading was practiced pursuant to the Act. That is all. There is no assertion that she was injured or even offended thereby or that she was compelled to accept, approve or confess agreement with any dogma or creed or even to listen when the Scriptures were read. . . . However . . . this child had graduated from the public schools before this appeal was taken to this Court. Obviously no decision we could render now would protect any rights she may once have had, and this Court does not sit to decide arguments after events have put them to rest.

The complaint is similarly niggardly of facts to support a taxpayer's grievance. . . . In this school the Bible is read, according to statute. There is no allegation that this activity is supported by any separate tax or paid for from any particular appropriation or that it adds any sum whatever to the cost of conducting the school. No information is given as to what kind of taxes are paid by appellants and there is no averment that the Bible reading increases any tax they do pay or that as taxpayers they are, will, or possibly can be out of pocket because of it.

It is apparent that the grievance which it is sought to litigate here is not a direct dollars-and-cents injury but is a religious difference. If appellants established the requisite special injury necessary to a taxpayer's case or controversy, it would not matter that their dominant inducement to action was more religious than mercenary. It is not a question of motivation but of possession of the requisite financial interest that is, or is threatened to be, injured by the unconstitutional conduct. We find no such direct and particular financial interest here. If the Act may give rise to a legal case or controversy on some behalf, the appellants cannot obtain a decision from this Court by a feigned issue of taxation.

ZORACH v. CLAUSON.

343 U. S. 306

Decided April 28, 1952 — three Justices dissenting.

Mr. Justice DOUGLAS delivered the opinion of the Court.

New York City has a program which permits its public schools to release students during the school day so that they may leave the school buildings and school grounds and go to religious centers for religious instruction or devotional exercises. A student is released on written request of his parents. Those not released stay in the classrooms. The churches make weekly reports to the schools, sending a list of children who have been released from public school but who have not reported for religious instruction.

This "released time" program involves neither religious instruction in public school classrooms nor the expenditure of public funds. . . . The case is therefore unlike *McCollum v. Board of Education*, 333 U. S. 203 . . .

Appellants, who are taxpayers and residents of New York City and whose children attend its public schools, challenge the present law, contending it is in essence not different from the one involved in the *McCollum* case. Their argument, stated elaborately in various ways, reduces itself to this: the weight and influence of the school is put behind a program for religious instruction; public school teachers police it, keeping tab on students who are released; the classroom activities come to a halt while the students who are released for religious instruction are on leave; the school is a crutch on which the churches are leaning for support in their religious training; without the cooperation of the schools this "released time" program, like the one in the *McCollum* case, would be futile and ineffective.

It takes obtuse reasoning to inject any issue of the "free exercise" of religion into the present case. No one is forced to go to the religious classroom and no religious exercise or instruction is brought to the classrooms of the public schools.

There is a suggestion that the system involves the use of coercion to get public school students into religious classrooms. There is no evidence in the record before us that supports that conclusion.

Moreover, apart from that claim of coercion, we do not see how New York by this type of "released time" program has made a law respecting an establishment of religion within the meaning of the First Amendment. . . . There cannot be the slightest doubt that the First Amendment reflects the philosophy that Chruch and State should be separated. And so far as interference with the "free exercise" of religion and an "establishment" of religion are concerned, the separation must be complete and unequivocal. The First Amendment within the scope of its coverage permits no exception; the prohibition is absolute. The First Amendment, however, does not say that in every and all respects there shall be a separation of Chruch and State. Rather, it studiously defines the manner, the specific ways, in which there shall be no concert or union or dependency one on the other. That is the common sense of the matter. Otherwise the state and religion would be aliens to each other — hostile, suspicious and even unfriendly. Churches could not be required to pay even property taxes. Municipalities would not be permitted to render police or fire protection to religious groups. Policemen who helped parishioners into their places of worship would violate the Constitution. Prayers in our legislative halls; the appeals to the Almighty in the messages of the Chief Executive; the proclamations making Thanksgiving Day a holiday; "so help me God" in our courtroom oaths — these and all other references to the Almighty that run through our laws, our public rituals, our ceremonies would be flouting the First Amendment. A fastidious atheist or agnostic could even object to the supplication with which the Court opens each session: "God save the United States and this Honorable Court."

We would have to press the concept of separation of Church and State to these extremes to condemn the present law on constitutional grounds. . . .A Catholic student applies to his teacher for permission to leave the school during hours on a Holy Day of Obligation to attend a mass. A Jewish student asks his teacher for permission to be excused for Yom Kippur. A Protestant wants the afternoon off for a family baptismal ceremony. In each case the teacher requires parental consent in writing. In each case the teacher, in order to make sure the student is not a truant, goes further and requires a report from the priest, the rabbi, or the minister. The teacher in other words cooperates in a religious program to the extent of making it possible for her students to participate in it. Whether she does it occasionally for a few students, regularly for one, or pursuant to a systematized program designed to further the religious needs of all the students does not alter the character of the act.

We are a religious people whose institutions presuppose a Supreme Being. We guarantee the freedom to worship as one chooses. We make room for as wide a variety of beliefs and creeds as the spiritual needs of man deem necessary. We sponsor an attitude on the part of government that shows no partiality to any one group and that lets each flourish according to the zeal of its adherents and the appeal of its dogma. When the state encourages religious instruction or cooperates with religious authorities by adjusting the schedule of public events to sectarian needs, it follows the best of our traditions. For it then respects the religious nature of our people and accommodates the public service to their spiritual needs. To hold that it may not would be to find in the Constitution a requirement that the government show a callous indifference to religious groups. That would be preferring those who believe in no religion over those who do believe. Government may not finance religious groups nor undertake religious instruction nor blend secular and sectarian education nor use secular institutions to force one or some religion on any person. But we find no constitutional requirement which makes it necessary for government to be hostile to religion and to throw its weight against efforts to widen the effective scope of religious influence. The government must be neutral when it comes to competition between sects. It may not thrust any sect on any person. It may not make a religious observance compulsory. It may not coerce anyone to attend church, to observe a religious holiday, or to take religious instruction. But it can close its doors or suspend its operations as to those who want to repair to their religious sanctuary for worship or instruction. No more than that is undertaken here.

We follow the *McCollum* case. But we cannot expand it to cover the present released time program unless separation of Chruch and State means that public institutions can make no adjustments of their schedules to accommodate the religious needs of the people. We cannot read into the Bill of Rights such a philosophy of hostility to religion.

Mr. Justice BLACK, dissenting.

I see no significant difference between the invalid Illinois system and that of New York here sustained. Except for the use of the school buildings in Illinois, there is no difference between the systems which I consider even worthy of mention. In the New York program, as in that of Illionis, the school authorities release some of the children on the condition that they attend the religious classes, get reports on whether they attend, and hold the other children in the school building until the religious hour is over. As we attempted to make categorically clear, the *McCollum* decision would have been the same if the religious classes had not been held in the school buildings.... *McCollum* ... held that Illinois could not constitutionally manipulate the compelled classroom hours of its compulsory school machinery so as to channel children into sectarian classes. Yet that is exactly what the Court holds New York can do.

Here the sole question is whether New York can use its compulsory education laws to help religious sects get attendants presumably too unenthusiastic to go unless moved to do so by the pressure of this state machinery. That this is the plan, purpose, design and consequence of the New York program cannot be denied. The state thus makes religious sects beneficiaries of its power to compel children to attend secular schools. Any use of such coercive power by the state to help or hinder some religious sects or to prefer all religious sects over nonbelievers or vice versa is just what I think the First Amendment forbids. In considering whether a state has entered this forbidden field the question is not whether it has entered too far but whether it has entered at all.

The Court's validation of the New York system rests in part on its statement that Americans are "a religious people whose institutions presuppose a Supreme Being." This was at least as true when the First Amendment was adopted; and it was just as true when eight Justices of this Court invalidated the released time system in *McCollum* on the premise that a state can no more "aid all religions" than it can aid one.... Now as then, it is only by wholly isolating the state from the religious sphere and compelling it to be completely neutral, that the freedom of each and every denomination and of all nonbelievers can be maintained.

The spiritual mind of man has thus been free to believe, disbelieve, or doubt, without repression, great or small, by the heavy hand of government. Statutes authorizing such repression have been stricken. Before today, our judicial opinions have refrained from drawing invidious distinctions between those who believe in no religion and those who do believe. The First Amendment has lost much if the religious follower and the atheist are no longer to be judicially regarded as entitled to equal justice under law.

State help to religion injects political and party prejudices into a holy field. It too often substitutes force for prayer, hate for love, and persecution for persuasion. Government should not be allowed, under cover of the soft euphemism of "co-operation," to steal into the sacred area of religious choice.

Mr. Justice FRANKFURTER, dissenting.

The Court tells us that in the maintenance of its public schools, "[The State government] can close its doors or suspend its operations" so that its citizens may be free for religious devotions or instruction. If that were the issue, it would not rise to the dignity of a constitutional controversy. Of course a State may provide that the classes in its schools shall be dismissed, for any reason, or no reason, on fixed days, or for special occasions. The essence of this case is that the school system did not "close its doors" and did not "suspend its operations". There is all the difference in the world between letting the children out of school and letting some of them out of school into religious classes.

The pith of the case is that formalized religious instruction is substituted for other school activity which those who do not participate in the released-time program are compelled to attend.

. . . the Court relies upon the absence from the record of evidence of coercion in the operation of the system. . . . But the Court disregards the fact that as the case comes to us, there could be no proof of coercion, for the appellants were not allowed to make proof of it. Appellants alleged that "The operation of the released time program has resulted and inevitably results in the exercise of pressure and coercion upon parents and children to secure attendance by the children for religious instruction." This allegation — that coercion was in fact present and is inherent in the system, no matter what disavowals might be made in the operating regulations — was denied by respondents.

If we are to decide this case on the present record, however, a strict adherence to the usage of courts in ruling on the sufficiency of pleadings would require us to take as admitted the facts pleaded in the appellants' complaint, including the fact of coercion, actual and inherent. . . . I cannot see how a finding that coercion was absent, deemed critical by this Court in sustaining the practice, can be made here, when appellants were prevented from making a timely showing of coercion because the courts below thought it irrelevant.

Mr. Justice JACKSON, dissenting.

This released time program is founded upon a use of the State's power of coercion, which, for me, determines its unconstitutionality. Stripped to its essentials, the plan has two stages, first, that the State compel each student to yield a large part of his time for public secular education and, second, that some of it be "released" to him on condition that he devote it to sectarian religious purposes.

The greater effectiveness of this system over voluntary attendance after school hours is due to the truant officer who, if the youngster fails to go to the Church school, dogs him back to the public schoolroom. Here schooling is more or less suspended during the "released time" so the nonreligious attendants will not forge ahead of the churchgoing absentees. But it serves as a temporary jail for a pupil who will not go to Church.

The day that this country ceases to be free for irreligion it will cease to be free for religion — except for the sect that can win political power. The same epithetical jurisprudence used by the Court today to beat down those who oppose pressuring children into some religion can devise as good epithets tomorrow against those who object to pressuring them into a favored religion.

ENGEL v. VITALE.

370 U. S. 421

Decided June 25, 1962 — one Justice dissenting.

Mr. Justice BLACK delivered the opinion of the Court.

The respondent Board of Education of Union Free School District No. 9, New Hyde Park, New York, acting in its official capacity under state law, directed the School District's principal to cause the following prayer to be said aloud by each class in the presence of a teacher at the beginning of each school day:

> "Almighty God, we acknowledge our dependence upon Thee, and we beg Thy blessings upon us, our parents, our teachers and our Country.

This daily procedure was adopted on the recommendation of the State Board of Regents, a governmental agency created by the State Constitution to which the New York Legislature has granted broad supervisory, executive, and legislative powers over the State's public school system.

Shortly after the practice of reciting the Regents' prayer was adopted by the School District, the parents of ten pupils brought this action in a New York State Court insisting that use of this official prayer in the public schools was contrary to the beliefs, religions, or religious practices of both themselves and their children. Among other things, these parents challenged the constitutionality of both the state law authorizing the School District to direct the use of prayer in public schools and the School District's regulation ordering the recitation of this particular prayer on the ground that these actions of official governmental agencies violate that part of the First Amendment of the Federal Constitution which commands that "Congress shall make no law respecting an establishment of religion" — a command which was "made applicable to the State of New York by the Fourteenth Amendment of the said Constitution."

We think that by using its public school system to encourage recitation of the Regents' prayer, the State of New York has adopted a practice wholly inconsistent with the Establishment Clause. There can, of course, be no doubt that New York's program of daily classroom invocation of God's blessings as prescribed in the Regents' prayer is a religious activity.

The petitioners contend among other things that the state laws requiring or permitting use of the Regents' prayer must be struck down as a violation of the Establishment Clause because that prayer was composed by governmental officials as a part of a governmental program to further religious beliefs. For this reason, petitioners argue, the State's use of the Regents' prayer in its public school system breaches the constitutional wall of separation between Church and State. We agree with that contention since we think that the constitutional prohibition against laws respecting an establishment of religion must at least mean that in this country it is no part of the business of government to compose official prayers for any group of the American people to recite as a part of a religious program carried on by government.

By the time of the adoption of the Constitution, our history shows that there was a widespread awareness among many Americans of the dangers of a union of Church and State. These people knew, some of them from bitter personal experience, that one of the greatest dangers to the freedom of the individual to worship in his own way lay in the Government's placing its official stamp of approval upon one particular kind of prayer or one particular form of religious services. . . . The First Amendment was added to the Constitution to stand as a guarantee that neither the power nor the prestige of the Federal Government would be used to control, support or influence the kinds of prayer the American people can say — that the people's religions must not be subjected to the pressures of government for change each time a new political administration is elected to office. Under that Amendment's prohibition against governmental establishment of religion, as reinforced by the provisions of the Fourteenth Amendment, government in this counrty, be it state or federal, is without power to prescribe by law any particular form of prayer which is to be used as an official prayer in carrying on any program of governmentally sponsored religious activity.

There can be no doubt that New York's state prayer program officially establishes the religious beliefs embodied in the Regents' prayer. The respondents' argument to the contrary, which is largely based upon the contention that the Regents' prayer is "nondenominational" and the fact that the program, as modified and approved by state courts, does not require all pupils to recite the prayer but permits those who wish to do so to remain silent or be excused from the room, ignores the essential nature of the program's constitutional defects. Neither the fact that the prayer may be denominationally neutral nor the fact that its observance on the part of the students is voluntary can serve to free it from the limitations of the Establishment Clause, as it might from the Free Exercise Clause, of the First Amendment, both of which are operative against the States by virtue of the Fourteenth Amendment. . . . The Establishment Clause, unlike the Free Exercise Clause, does not depend upon any showing of direct governmental compulsion and is violated by the enactment of laws which establish an official religion whether those laws operate directly to coerce nonobserving individuals or not. . . . When the power, prestige and financial support of government is placed behind a particular religious belief, the indirect coercive pressure upon religious minorities to conform to the prevailing officially approved religion is plain. But the purposes underlying the Establishment Clause go much further than that. Its first and most immediate purpose rested on the belief that a union of government and religion tends to destroy government and to degrade religion. . . . The Establishment Clause thus stands as an expression of principle on the part of the Founders of our Constitution that religion is too personal, too sacred, too holy, to permit its "unhallowed perversion" by a civil magistrate. Another purpose of the Establishment Clause rested upon an awareness of the historical fact that governmentally established religions and religious persecutions go hand in hand.

... It was in large part to get completely away from this sort of systematic religious persecution that the Founders brought into being our Nation, our Constitution, and our Bill of Rights with its prohibition against any governmental establishment of religion. The New York laws officially prescribing the Regents' prayer are inconsistent both with the purposes of the Establishment Clause and with the Establishment Clause itself.

It has been argued that to apply the Constitution in such a way as to prohibit state laws respecting an establishment of religious services in public schools is to indicate a hostility toward religion or toward prayer. Nothing, of course, could be more wrong. The history of man is inseparable from the history of religion. And perhaps it is not too much to say that since the beginning of that history many people have devoutly believed that "More things are wrought by prayer than this world dreams of.".... And there were men of this same faith in the power of prayer who led the fight for adoption of our Constitution and also for our Bill of Rights with the very guarantees of religious freedom that forbid the sort of governmental activity which New York has attempted here. These men knew that the First Amendment, which tried to put an end to governmental control of religion and of prayer, was not written to destroy either.

To those who may subscribe to the view that because the Regents' official prayer is so brief and general there can be no danger to religious freedom in its governmental establishment, however, it may be appropriate to say in the words of James Madison, the author of the First Amendment:

> "[I]t is proper to take alarm at the first experiment on our liberties.... Who does not see that the same authority which can establish Christianity, in exclusion of all other Religions, may establish with the same ease any particular sect of Christians, in exclusion of all other Sects? That the same authority which can force a citizen to contribute three pence only of his property for the support of any one establishment, may force him to conform to any other establishment in all cases whatsoever?"

SCHOOL DISTRICT OF ABINGTON TOWNSHIP, PENNSYLVANIA v. SCHEMPP.

MURRAY v. CURLETT.

374 U. S. 203

Decided June 17, 1963 — one Justice dissenting.

Mr. Justice CLARK delivered the opinion of the Court.

Once again we are called upon to consider the scope of the provision of the First Amendment to the United States Constitution which declares that "Congress shall make no law respecting an establishment of religion, or prohibiting the free exercise thereof. . ." These companion cases present the issues in the context of state action requiring that schools begin each day with readings from the Bible. While raising the basic questions under slightly different factual situations, the cases permit of joint treatment. In light of the history of the First Amendment and of our cases interpreting and applying its requirements, we hold that the practices at issue and the laws requiring them are unconstitutional under the Establishment Clause, as applied to the States through the Fourteenth Amendment.

The Commonwealth of Pennsylvania by law . . . requires that "At least ten verses from the Holy Bible shall be read, without comment, at the opening of each public school on each school day. Any child shall be excused from such Bible reading, or attending such Bible reading, upon the written request of his parent or guardian." The Schempp family, husband and wife and two of their three children, brought suit to enjoin enforcement of the statute, contending that their rights under the Fourteenth Amendment to the Constitution of the United States are, have been, and will continue to be violated unless this statute be declared unconstitutional as violative of these provisions of the First Amendment.

On each school day at the Abington Senior High School between 8:15 and 8:30 a.m., while the pupils are attending their home rooms or advisory sections, opening exercises are conducted pursuant to the statute. The exercises are broadcast into each room in the school building through an intercommunications system and are conducted under the supervision of a teacher by students attending the school's radio and television workshop. Selected students from this course gather each morning in the school's workshop studio for the exercises, which include readings by one of the students of 10 verses of the Holy Bible, broadcast to each room in the building. This is followed by the recitation of the Lord's Prayer . . . Participation in the opening exercises, as directed by the statute, is voluntary. The student reading the verses from the Bible may select the passages and read from any version he chooses, although the only copies furnished by the school are the King James version . . . During the period in which the exercises have been conducted the King James, the Douay and the Revised Standard versions of the Bible have been used, as well as the Jewish Holy Scriptures. There are no prefatory statements, no questions asked or solicited, no comments or explanations made and no interpretations given at or during the exercises. The students and parents are advised that the student may absent himself from the classroom or, should he elect to remain, not participate in the exercises.

In 1905 the Board of School Commissioners of Baltimore City adopted a rule . . . provided for the holding of opening exercises in the schools of the city, consisting primarily of the "reading, without comment, of a chapter in the Holy Bible and/or the use of the Lord's Prayer." The petitoners, Mrs. Madalyn Murray and her son, William J. Murray III, are both professed atheists. Following unsuccessful attempts to have the respondent school board rescind the rule, this suit was filed for mandamus to compel its rescission and cancellation. It was alleged that William was a student in a public school of the city and Mrs. Murray, his mother, was a taxpayer therein; that it was the practice under the rule to have a reading on each school morning from the King James version of the Bible; that at petitioners' insistence the rule was amended to permit children to be excused from the exercises on request of the parent and that William had been excused pursuant thereto; that nevertheless the rule as amended was in violation of the petitioners' rights "to freedom of religion under the First and Fourteenth Amendments" and in violation of "the principle of separation between church and state, contained therein. . . ." The petition particularized the petitioners' atheistic beliefs and stated that the rule, as practiced, violated their rights

> "in that it threatens their religious liberty by placing a premium on belief as against non-belief and subjects their freedom of conscience to the rule of the majority; it pronounces belief in God as the source of all moral and spiritual values, equating these values with religious values, and thereby renders sinister, alien and suspect the beliefs and ideals of your Petitioners, promotiong doubt and question of their morality, good citizenship and good faith."

It is true that religion has been closely identified with our history and government. . . . The fact that the Founding Fathers believed devotedly that there was a God and that the unalienable rights of man were rooted in Him is clearly evidenced in their writings, from the Mayflower Compact to the Constitution itself. This background is evidenced today in our public life through the continuance in our oaths of office from the Presidency to the Alderman of the final supplication, "So help me God." Likewise each House of the Congress provides through its Chaplain an opening prayer, and the sessions of this Court are declared open by the crier in a short ceremony, the final phrase of which invokes the grace of God. . . . Indeed, only last year an official survey of the country indicated that 64% of our people have church membership . . . while less than 3% profess no religion whatever.

This is not to say, however, that religion has been so identified with our history and government that religious freedom is not likewise as strongly imbedded in our public and private life. . . . This freedom to worship was indispensable in a country whose people came from the four quarters of the earth and brought with them a diversity of religious opinion. Today authorities list 83 separate religious bodies, each with membership exceeding 50,000, existing among our people, as well as innumerable smaller groups.

First, this Court has decisively settled that the First Amendment's mandate that "Congress shall make no law respecting an establishment of religion, or prohibiting the free exercise thereof" has been made wholly applicable to the States by the Fourteenth Amendment.

Second, this Court has rejected unequivocally the contention that the Establishment Clause forbids only governmental preference of one religion over another.

While none of the parties to either of these cases has questioned these basic conclusions of the Court, both of which have been long established, recognized and consistently reaffirmed, others continue to question their history, logic and efficacy. Such contentions, in the light of the consistent interpretation in cases of this Court, seem entirely untenable and of value only as academic exercises.

The wholesome "neutrality" of which this Court's cases speak . . . stems from a recognition of the teachings of history that powerful sects or groups might bring about a fusion of governmental and religious functions or a concert or dependency of one upon the other to the end that official support of the State or Federal Government would be placed behind the tenets of one or of all orthodoxies. This the Establishment Clause prohibits. And a further reason for neutrality is found in the Free Exercise Clause, which recognizes the value of religious training, teaching and observance and, more particularly, the right of every person to freely choose his own course with reference thereto, free of any compulsion from the state. This the Free Exercise Clause guarantees. Thus, as we have seen, the two clauses may overlap. As we have indicated, the Establishment Clause has been directly considered by this Court eight times in the past score of years and, with only one Justice dissenting on the point, it has consistently held that the clause withdrew all legislative power respecting religious belief or the expression thereof. The test may be stated as follows: what are the purpose and the primary effect of the enactment? If either is the advancement or inhibition of religion then the enactment exceeds the scope of legislative power as circumscribed by the Constitution. That is to say that to withstand the strictures of the Establishment Clause there must be a secular legislative purpose and a primary effect that neither advances nor inhibits religion. . . . The Free Exercise Clause, likewise considered many times here, withdraws from legislative power, state and federal, the exertion of any restraint on the free exercise of religion. Its purpose is to secure religious liberty in the individual by prohibiting any invasions thereof by civil authority. Hence it is necessary in a free exercise case for one to show the coercive effect of the enactment as it operates against him in the practice of his religion. The distinction between the two clauses is apparent — a violation of the Free Exercise Clause is predicated on coercion while the Establishment Clause violation need not be so attended.

Applying the Establishment Clause principles to the cases at bar we find that the States are requiring the selection and reading at the opening of the school day of verses from the Holy Bible and the recitation of the Lord's Prayer by the students in unision.

The conclusion follows that in both cases the laws require religious exercises and such exercises are being conducted in direct violation of the rights of the appellees and petitioners. Nor are these required exercises mitigated by the fact that individual students may absent themselves upon parental request, for that fact furnishes no defense to a claim of unconstitutionality under the Establishment Clause. . . . Further, it is no defense to urge that the religious practices here may be relatively minor encroachments on the First Amendment. The breach of neutrality that is today a trickling stream may all too soon become a raging torrent . . .

It is insisted that unless these religious exercises are permitted a "religion of secularism" is established in the schools. We agree of course that the State may not establish a "religion of secularism" in the sense of affirmatively opposing or showing hostility to religion, thus "preferring those who believe in no religion over those who do believe.". . . We do not agree, however, that this decision in any sense has that effect. In addition, it might well be said that one's education is not complete without a study of comparative religion or the history of religion and its relationship to the advancement of civilization. It certainly may be said that the Bible is worthy of study for its literary and historic qualities. Nothing we have said here indicates that such study of the Bible or of religion, when presented objectively as part of a secular program of education, may not be effected consistently with the First Amendment. But the exercises here do not fall into those categories. They are religious exercises, required by the States in violation of the command of the First Amendment that the Government maintain strict neutrality, neither aiding nor opposing religion.

Finally, we cannot accept that the concept of neutrality, which does not permit a State to require a religious exercise even with the consent of the majority of those effected, collides with the majority's right to free exercise of religion. While the Free Exercise Clause clearly prohibits the use of state action to deny the rights of free exercise to *anyone*, it has never meant that a majority could use the machinery of the State to practice its beliefs.

The place of religion in our society is an exalted one, achieved through a long tradition of reliance on the home, the church and the inviolable citadel of the individual heart and mind. We have come to recognize through bitter experience that it is not within the power of government to invade that citadel, whether its purpose or effect be to aid or oppose, to advance or retard. In the relationship between man and religion, the State is firmly committed to a position of neutrality. Though the application of that rule requires interpretation of a delicate sort, the rule itself is clearly and concisely stated in the words of the First Amendment.

Mr. Justice DOUGLAS, concurring.

These regimes violate the Establishment Clause in two different ways. In each case the State is conducting a religious exercise; and, as the Court holds, that cannot be done without violating the "neutrality" required of the State by the balance of power between individual, church and state that has been struck by the First Amendment. But the Establishment Clause is not limited to precluding the State itself from conducting religious exercises. It also forbids the State to employ its facilities or funds in a way that gives any church, or all churches, greater strength in our society than it would have by relying on its members alone. Thus, the present regimes must fall under that clause for the additional reason that public funds, though small in amount, are being used to promote a religious exercise. Through the mechanism of the State, all of the people are being required to finance a religious exercise that only some of the people want and that violates the sensibilities of others.

The most effective way to establish any institution is to finance it; and this truth is reflected in the appeals by church groups for public funds to finance their religious schools. Financing a church either in its strictly religious activities or in its other activities is equally unconstitutional . . .

It is not the amount of public funds expended; as this case illustrates, it is the use to which public funds are put that is controlling. For the First Amendment does not say that some forms of establishment are allowed; it says that "no law respecting an establishment of religion" shall be made. What may not be done directly may not be done indirectly lest the Establishment Clause become a mockery.

Mr. Justice BRENNAN, concurring.

Americans regard the public schools as a most vital civic institution for the preservation of a democratic system of government. It is therefore understandable that the constitutional prohibitions encounter their severest test when they are sought to be applied in the school classroom. Nevertheless it is this Court's inescapable duty to declare whether exercises in the public schools of the States, such as those of Pennsylvania and Maryland questioned here, are involvements of religion in public institutions of a kind which offends the First and Fourteenth Amendments.

The fact is that the line which separates the secular from the sectarian in American life is elusive. The difficulty of defining the boundary with precision inheres in a paradox central to our scheme of liberty. While our institutions reflect a firm conviction that we are a religious people, those institutions by solemn constitutional injunction may not officially involve religion in such a way as to prefer, discriminate against, or oppress, a particular sect or religion. Equally the Constitution enjoins those involvements of religious with secular institutions which (a) serve the essentially religious activities of religious institutions; (b) employ the organs of government for essentially religious purposes; or (c) use essentially religious means to serve governmental ends where secular means would suffice.

The reasons we gave only last term in *Engel v. Vitale*, 370 U. S. 421, for finding in the New York Regents' prayer an impermissible establishment of religion, compel the same judgment of the practices at bar.... It should be unnecessary to observe that our holding does not declare that the First Amendment manifests hostility to the practice or teaching of religion, but only applies prohibitions incorporated in the Bill of Rights in recognition of historic needs shared by Church and State alike.

Plainly, the Establishment Clause, in the contemplation of the Framers, "did not limit the constitutional proscription to any particular, dated form of state-supported theological venture." "What Virginia had long practiced, and what Madison, Jefferson and others fought to end, was the extension of civil government's support to religion in a manner which made the two in some degree interdependent, and thus threatened the freedom of each. The purpose of the Establishment Clause was to assure that the national legislature would not exert its power in the service of any purely religious end; that it would not, as Virignia and virtually all of the Colonies had done, make of religion, as religion, an object of legislation. . . . The Establishment Clause withdrew from the sphere of legitimate legislative concern and competence a specific, but comprehensive, area of human conduct: man's belief or disbelief in the verity of some transcendental idea and man's expression in action of that belief or disbeief." *McGowan v. Maryland* . . . 366 U. S., at 465-466 . . .

In sum, the history which our prior decisions have summoned to aid interpretation of the Establishment Clause permits little doubt that its prohibition was designed comprehensively to prevent those official involvements of religion which would tend to foster or discourage religious worship or belief.

But an awareness of history and an appreciation of the aims of the Founding Fathers do not always resolve concrete problems. . . . A more fruitful inquiry, it seems to me, is whether the practices here challenged threaten those consequences which the Framers deeply feared; whether, in short, they tend to promote that type of interdependence between religion and state which the First

Amendment was designed to prevent.

A too literal quest for the advice of the Founding Fathers upon the issues of these cases seems to me futile and misdirected for several reasons: First, on our precise problem the historical record is at best ambigious, and statements can readily be found to support either side of the proposition.

Second, the structure of American education has greatly changed since the First Amendment was adopted. In the context of our modern emphasis upon public education available to all citizens, any views of the eighteenth century as to whether the exercises at bar are an "establishment" offer little aid to decision.

Third, our religious composition makes us a vastly more diverse people than were our forefathers. They knew differences chiefly among Protestant sects. Today the Nation is far more heterogeneous religiously, including as it does substantial minorities not only of Catholics and Jews but as well of those who worship according to no version of the Bible and those who worship no God at all.

Fourth, the American experiment in free public education available to all children has been guided in large measure by the dramatic evolution of the religious diversity among the population which our public schools serve. The interaction of these two important forces in our national life has placed in bold relief certain positive values in the consistent application to public institutions generally, and public schools particularly, of the constitutional decree against official involvements of religion which might produce the evils the Framers meant the Establishment Clause to forestall. . . . It is implicit in the history and character of American public education that the public schools serve a uniquely *public* function: the training of American citizens in an atmosphere free of parochial, divisive, or separatist influences of any sort — an atmosphere in which children may assimilate a heritage common to all American groups and religions. . . . This is a heritage neither theistic nor atheistic, but simply civic and patriotic.

Attandance at the public schools has never been compulsory; parents remain morally and constitutionally free to choose the academic environment in which they wish their children to be educated. . . . The choice which is thus preserved is between a public secular education with its uniquely democratic values, and some form of private or sectarian education, which offers values of its own. In my judgment the First Amendment forbids the State to inhibit that freedom of choice by diminishing the attractiveness of either alternative . . . The lesson of history . . . is that a system of free public education forfeits its unique contribution to the growth of democratic citizenship when that choice ceases to be freely available to each parent.

The issue of what particular activities the Establishment Clause forbids the States to undertake is our more immediate concern. . . . a careful study of the relevant history led the Court to the view, consistently recognized in decisions since *Everson*, that the Establishment Clause embodied the Framers' conclusion that government and religion have discreet interests which are mutually best served when each avoids too close a proximity to the other. It is not only the nonbeliever who fears the injection of sectarian doctrines and controversies into the civil polity, but in as high degree it is the devout believer who fears the secularization of a creed which becomes too deeply involved with and dependent upon the government. It has rightly been said of the history of the Establishment Clause that "our tradition of civil liberty rests not only on the secularism of a Thomas Jefferson but also on the fervent sectarianism . . . of a Roger Williams."

Our decisions on questions of religious education or exercises in the public schools have consistently reflected this dual aspect of the Establishment Clause.

The use of prayers and Bible readings at the opening of the school day long antedates the founding of our Republic.

After the Revolution, the new States uniformly continued these long-established practices in the private and the few public grammar schools. . . . As the free public schools gradually supplanted the private academies and sectarian schools between 1800 and 1850, morning devotional exercises were retained with few alterations.

Statutory provision for daily religious exercises is, however, of quite recent origin. At the turn of this century, there was but one State — Massachusetts — which had a law making morning prayer or Bible reading obligatory. Statutes elsewhere either permitted such practices or simply left the question to local option. It was not until after 1910 that 11 more States, within a few years joined Massachusetts in making one or both exercises compulsory. . . . In no State has there ever been a constitutional or statutory prohibition against the recital of prayers or the reading of Scripture, although a number of States have outlawed these practices by judicial decision or administrative order. What is noteworthy about the panoply of state and local regulations from which these cases emerge is the relative recency of the statutory codification of practices which have ancient roots, and the rather small number of States which have ever prescribed compulsory religious exercises in the public schools.

The purposes underlying the adoption and perpetuation of these practices are somewhat complex. It is beyond question that the religious benefits and values realized from daily prayer and Bible reading have usually been considered paramount, and sufficient to justify the continuation of such practices.

Almost from the beginning religious exercises in the public schools have been the subject of intense criticism, vigorous debate, and judicial or administrative prohibition. Significantly, educators and school boards early entertained doubts about both the legality and the soundness of opening the school day with compulsory prayer or Bible reading.

Thus the panorama of history permits no other conclusion than that daily prayers and Bible readings in the public schools have always been designed to be, and have been regarded as, essentially religious exercises. Unlike the Sunday closing laws, these exercises appear neither to have been divorced from their religious origins nor deprived of their centrally religious character by the passage of time. . . . On this distinction alone we might well rest a constitutional decision. But three further contentions have been pressed in the argument of these cases.

First, it is argued that however clearly religious may have been the origins and early nature of daily prayer and Bible reading, these practices today serve so clearly secular educational purposes that their religious attributes may be overlooked.

The secular purposes which devotional exercises are said to serve fall into two categories — those which depend upon an immediately religious experience shared by the participating children; and those which appear sufficiently divorced from the religious content of the devotional material that they can be served equally by nonreligious materials. With respect to the first objective . . . To the extent that only *religious* materials will serve this purpose, it seems to me that the purpose as well as the means is so plainly religious that the exercise is necessarily forbidden by the Establishment Clause.

The second justification assumes that religious exercises at the start of the school day may directly serve solely secular ends . . . It has not been shown that readings from the speeches and messages of great Americans, for example, or from the documents of our heritage of liberty, daily recitation of the Pledge of Allegiance, or even the observance of a moment of reverent silence at the opening of class, may not adequately serve the solely secular purposes of the devotional activities without jeopardizing either the religious liberties of any members of the community or the proper degree of separation between the spheres of religion and government.

Second, it is argued that the particular practices involved in the two cases before us are unobjectionable because they prefer no particular sect or sects at the expense of others. . . . To vary the version as the Abington and Baltimore schools have done may well be less offensive than to read from the King James version every day, as once was the practice. But the result even of this relatively benign procedure is that majority sects are preferred in approximate proportion to their representation in the community and in the student body, while the smaller sects suffer commensurate discrimination.

The argument contains, however, a more basic flaw. There are persons in every community — often deeply devout — to whom any version of the Judaeo-Christian Bible is offensive. There are others whose reverence for the Holy Scriptures demands private study or reflection and to whom public reading or recitation is sacrilegious . . .

It has been suggested that a tentative solution to these problems may lie in the fashioning of a "common core" of theology tolerable to all creeds but preferential to none. But as one commentator has recently observed, "[h]istory is not encouraging to" those who hope to fashion a "common denominator of religion detached from its manifestation in any organized church.". . . *Engel* is surely authority that nonsectarian religious practices, equally with sectarian exercises, violate the Establishment Clause. Moreover, even if the Establishment Clause were oblivious to nonsectarian religious practices, I think it quite likely that the "common core" approach would be sufficiently objectionable to many groups to be foreclosed by the prohibitions of the Free Exercise Clause.

A third element which is said to absolve the practices involved in these cases from the ban of the religious guarantees of the Constitution is the provision to excuse or exempt students who wish not to participate. . . . the short, and to me sufficient, answer is that the availability of excusal or exemption simply has no relevance to the establishment question, if it is once found that these practices are essentially religious exercises designed at least in part to achieve religious aims through the use of public school facilities during the school day.

. . . the excusal procedure itself necessarily operates in such a way as to infringe the rights of free exercise of those children who wish to be excused. We have held in *Barnette* and *Torcaso*, respectively, that a State may require neither public school students nor candidates for an office of public trust to profess beliefs offensive to religious principles. By the same token the State could not constitutionally require a student to profess publicly his disbelief as the prerequisite to the exercise of his constitutional right of abstention. . . . by requiring what is tantamount in the eyes of teachers and schoolmates to a profession of disbelief, or at least of nonconformity, the procedure may well deter those children who do not wish to participate for any reason based upon the dictates of conscience from exercising an indisputably constitutional right to be excused. Thus the excusal provision in its operation subjects them to a cruel dilemma. In consequence, even devout children may well avoid claiming their right and simply continue to participate in exercises distasteful to them because of an understandable reluctance to be stigmatized as atheists or nonconformists simply on the basis of their request.

Such reluctance to seek exemption seems all the more likely in view of the fact that children are disinclined at this age to step out of line or to flout "peer-group norms."

These considerations bring me to a final contention of the school officials in these cases: that the invalidation of the exercises at bar permits this Court no alternative but to declare unconstitutional every vestige, however slight, of cooperation or accommodation between religion and government. I cannot accept that contention. . . . Our decision in these cases does not clearly forecast anything about the constitutionality of other types of interdependence between religious and other public institutions.

What the Framers meant to foreclose, and what our decisions under the Establishment Clause have forbidden, are those involvements of religious with secular institutions which (a) serve the essentially religious activities of religious institutions; (b) employ the organs of government for essentially religious purposes; or (c) use essentially religious means to serve governmental ends, where secular means would suffice. . . . On the other hand, there may be myriad forms of involvements of government with religion which do not import such dangers and therefore should not, in my judgment, be deemed to violate the Establishment Clause. Nothing in the Constitution compels the organs of government to be blind to what everyone else perceives — that religious differences among Americans have important and pervasive implications for our society. Likewise nothing in the Establishment Clause forbids the application of legislation having purely secular ends in such a way as to alleviate burdens upon the free exercise of an individual's religious beliefs.

The holding of the Court today plainly does not foreclose teaching *about* the Holy Scriptures or about the differences between religious sects in classes in literature or history. Indeed, whether or not the Bible is involved, it would be impossible to teach meaningfully many subjects in the social sciences or the humanities without some mention of religion. To what extent, and at what points in the curriculum, religious materials should be cited are matters which the courts ought to entrust very largely to the experienced officials who superintend our Nation's public schools. They are experts in such matters, and we are not.

Mr. Justice GOLDBERG, with whom Mr. Justice HARLAN joins, concurring.

It is said, and I agree, that the attitude of government toward religion must be one of neutrality. But untutored devotion to the concept of neutrality can lead to invocation or approval of results which partake not simply of that noninterference and noninvolvement with the religious which the Constitution commands, but of a brooding and pervasive devotion to the secular and a passive, or even active, hostility to the religious. Such results are not only not compelled by the Constitution, but, it seems to me, are prohibited by it.

Government must inevitably take cognizance of the existence of religion and, indeed, under certain circumstances the First Amendment may require that it do so. And it seems clear to me from the opinions in the present and past cases that the Court would recognize the propriety of providing military chaplains and of the teaching *about* religion, as distinguished from the teaching *of* religion, in the public schools. The examples could readily be multiplied, for both the required and the permissible accommodations between state and church frame the relation as one free of hostility or favor and productive of religious and political harmony, but without undue involvement of one in the concerns or practices of the other.

The practices here involved do not fall within any sensible or acceptable concept of compelled or permitted accommodation and involve the state so significantly and directly in the realm of the sectarian as to give rise to those very divisive influences and inhibitions of freedom which both religion clauses of the First Amendment preclude. . . . The pervasive religiosity and direct governmental involvement inhering in the prescription of prayer and Bible reading in the public schools, during and as part of the curricular day, involving young impressionable children whose school attendance is statutorily compelled, and utilizing the prestige, power, and influence of school administration, staff, and authority, cannot realistically be termed simply accommodation, and must fall within the interdiction of the First Amendment. . . . The First Amendment does not prohibit practices which by any realistic measure create none of the dangers which it is designed to prevent and which do not so directly or substantially involve the state in religious exercises or in the favoring of religion as to have meaningful and practical impact. It is of course true that great consequences can grow from small beginnings, but the measure of constitutional adjudication is the ability and willingness to distinguish between real threat and mere shadow.

Mr. Justice STEWART, dissenting.

The First Amendment declares that "Congrss shall make no law respecting an establishment of religion, or prohibiting the free exercise thereof . . ." It is, I think, a fallacious oversimplification to regard these two provisions as establishing a single constitutional standard of "separation of church and state," which can be mechanically applied in every case to delineate the required boundaries between government and religion. We err in the first place if we do not recognize, as a matter of history and as a matter of the imperatives of our free society, that religion and government must necessarily interact in countless ways. Secondly, the fact is that while in many contexts the Establishment Clause and the Free Exercise Clause fully complement each other, there are areas in which a doctrinaire reading of the Establishment Clause leads to irreconcilable conflict with the Free Exercise Clause.

As a matter of history, the First Amendment was adopted solely as a limitation upon the newly created National Government. . . . Each State was left free to go its own way and pursue its own policy with respect to religion.

So matters stood until the adoption of the Fourteenth Amendment, or more accurately, until this Court's decision in *Cantwell v. Connecticut*, in 1940, 310 U. S. 296.

That the central value embodied in the First Amendment — and, more particularly, in the guarantee of "liberty" contained in the Fourteenth — is the safeguarding of an individual's right to free exercise of his religion has been consistently recognized.

It is this concept of constitutional protection embodied in our decisions which makes the cases before us such difficult ones for me. For there is involved in these cases a substantial free exercise claim on the part of those who affirmatively desire to have their children's school day open with the reading of passages from the Bible.

For a compulsory state educational system so structures a child's life that if religious exercises are held to be an impermissible activity in schools, religion is placed at an artificial and state-created disadvantage. Viewed in this light, permission of such exercises for those who want them is necessary if the schools are truly to be neutral in the matter of religion.

What seems to me to be of paramount importance, then, is recognition of the fact that the claim advanced here in favor of Bible reading is sufficiently substantial to make simple reference to the constitutional phrase "establishment of religion" as inadequate an analysis of the cases before us as the ritualistic invocation of the nonconstitutional phrase "separation of church and state." What these cases compel, rather, is an analysis of just what the "neutrality" is which is required by the interplay of the Establishment and Free Exercise Clauses of the First Amendment, as imbedded in the Fourteenth.

In the absence of evidence that the legislature or school board intended to prohibit local schools from substituting a different set of readings where parents requested such a change, we should not assume that the provisions before us — as actually administered — may not be construed simply as authorizing religious exercises, nor that the designations may not be treated simply as indications of the promulgating body's view as to the community's preference.

In the absence of coercion upon those who do not wish to participate . . . such provisions cannot, in my view, be held to represent the type of support of religion barred by the Establishment Clause. For the only support which such rules provide for religion is the withholding of state hostility . . .

. . . the question presented is not whether exercises such as those at issue here are constitutionally compelled, but rather whether they are constitutionally invalid. And that issue, in my view, turns on the question of coercion.

The governmental neutrality which the First and Fourteenth Amendments require in the cases before us, in other words, is the extension of evenhanded treatment to all who believe, doubt, or disbelieve — a refusal on the part of the State to weight the scales of private choice. In these cases, therefore, what is involved is not state action based on impermissible categories, but rather an attempt by the State to accommodate those differences which the existence in our society of a variety of religious beliefs makes inevitable. The Constitution requires that such efforts be struck down only if they are proven to entail the use of the secular authority of government to coerce a preference among such beliefs.

Both cases involve provisions which explicitly permit any student who wishes, to be excused from participation in the exercises. There is no evidence in either case as to whether there would exist any coercion of any kind upon a student who did not want to participate.

What our Constitition indispensably protects is the freedom of each of us, be he Jew or Agnostic, Christian or Atheist, Buddhist or Freethinker, to believe or disbelieve, to worship or not worship, to pray or keep silent, according to his own conscience, uncoerced and unrestrained by government.

CHAMBERLIN v. DADE COUNTY, BOARD OF PUBLIC INSTRUCTION.

377 U. S. 402

Decided June 1, 1964.

PER CURIAM.

The judgment of the Florida Supreme Court is reversed with respect to the issues of the constitutionality of prayer, and of devotional Bible reading pursuant to a Florida statute . . . in the public schools of Dade County. . . . As to the other questions raised, the appeal is dismissed for want of properly presented federal questions.

Mr. Justice DOUGLAS, with whom Mr. Justice BLACK agrees, concurring in part.

The "other questions raised" which the Court refuses to consider because not "properly presented" involve the constitutionality under the First and Fourteenth Amendments of baccalaureate services in the schools, a religious census among pupils, and a religious test for teachers.

I think, however, that two of those "other questions" — the baccaluareate services and the religious census — do not present substantial federal questions, and so I concur in the dismissal of the appeal as to them. As to the religious test for teachers, I think a substantial question is presented.

EPPERSON v. ARKANSAS.

393 U. S. 97

Decided November 12, 1968.

Mr. Justice FORTAS delivered the opinion of the Court.

This appeal challenges the constitutionality of the "anti-evolution" statute which the State of Arkansas adopted in 1928 to prohibit the teaching in its public schools and universities of the theory that man evolved from other species of life.

The Arkansas law makes it unlawful for a teacher in any state-supported school or university "to teach the theory or doctrine that mankind ascended or descended from a lower order of animals," or "to adopt or use in any such institution a textbook that teaches" this theory.

According to the testimony, until the events here in litigation, the official textbook furnished for the high school biology course did not have a section on the Darwinian Theory. Then, for the academic year 1965-1966, the school administration, on recommendation of the teachers of biology in the school system, adopted and prescribed a textbook which contained a chapter setting forth "the theory about the origin . . . of man from a lower form of animal."

Susan Epperson . . . was employed by the Little Rock school system in the fall of 1964 to teach 10th grade biology at Central High School. At the start of the next academic year, 1965, she was confronted by the new textbook . . . She faced at least a literal dilemma because she was supposed to use the new textbook for classroom instruction and presumably to teach the statutorily condemned chapter; but to do so would be a criminal offense and subject her to dismissal.

She instituted the present action . . . seeking a declaration that the Arkansas statute is void and enjoining the State and the defendant officials of the Little Rock school system from dismissing her for violation of the statute's provisions.

It is of no moment whether the law is deemed to prohibit mention of Darwin's theory, or to forbid any or all of the infinite varieties of communication embraced within the term "teaching." Under either interpretation, the law must be stricken because of its conflict with the constitutional prohibition of state laws respecting an establishment of religion or prohibiting the free exercise thereof. The overriding fact is that Arkansas' law selects from the body of knowledge a particular segment which it proscribes for the sole reason that it is deemed to conflict with a particular religious doctrine; that is, with a particular interpretation of the Book of Genesis by a particular religious group.

Government in our democracy, state and national, must be neutral in matters of religious theory, doctrine, and practice. It may not be hostile to any religion or to the advocacy of no-religion; and it may not aid, foster, or promote one religion or religious theory against another or even against the militant opposite. The First Amendment mandates governmental neutrality between religion and religion, and between religion and nonreligion.

Judicial interposition in the operation of the public school system of the Nation raises problems requiring care and restraint. Our courts, however, have not failed to apply the First Amendment's mandate in our educational system where essential to safeguard the fundamental values of freedom of speech and inquiry and of belief. By and large, public education in our Nation is committed to the control of state and local authorities. Courts do not and cannot intervene in the resolution of conflicts which arise in the daily operation of school systems and which do not directly and sharply implicate basic constitutional values. On the other hand, "[t]he vigilant protection of constitutional freedoms is nowhere more vital than in the community of American schools," *Shelton v. Tucker*, 364 U. S. 479, 487 (1960).

There is and can be no doubt that the First Amendment does not permit the State to require that teaching and learning must be tailored to the principles or prohibitions of any religious sect or dogma.

While study of religions and of the Bible from a literary and historic viewpoint, presented objectively as part of a secular program of education, need not collide with the First Amendment's prohibition, the State may not adopt programs or practices in its public schools or colleges which "aid or oppose" any religion. . . . This prohibition is absolute. It forbids alike the preference of a religious doctrine or the prohibition of theory which is deemed antagonistic to a particular dogma.

The State's undoubted right to prescribe the curriculum for its public schools does not carry with it the right to prohibit, on pain of criminal penalty, the teaching of a scientific theory or doctrine where that prohibition is based upon reasons that violate the First Amendment.

It is clear that fundamentalist sectarian conviction was and is the law's reason for existence.

Arkansas' law cannot be defended as an act of religious neutrality. Arkansas did not seek to excise from the curricula of its schools and universities all discussion of the origin of man. The law's effort was confined to an attempt to blot out a particular theory because of its supposed conflict with the Biblical account, literally read. Plainly, the law is contrary to the mandate of the First, and in violation of the Fourteenth, Amendment to the Constitution.

Mr. Justice BLACK, concurring.

It seems to me that in this situation the statute is too vague for us to strike it down on any ground but that: vagueness. Under this statute as construed by the Arkansas Supreme Court, a teacher cannot know whether he is forbidden to mention Darwin's theory, at all or only free to discuss it as long as he rafrains from contending that it is true. It is an established rule that a statute which leaves an ordinary man so doubtful about its meaning that he cannot know when he has violated it denies him the first essential of due process. . . . Holding the statute too vague to enforce would not only follow long-standing constitutional precedents but it would avoid having this Court take unto itself the duty of a State's highest court to interpret and mark the boundaries of the State's laws. And, more important, it would not place this Court in the unenviable position of violating the principle of leaving the States absolutely free to choose their own curriculums for their own schools so long as their action does not palpably conflict with a clear constitutional command.

I find it difficult to agree with the Court's statement that "there can be no doubt that Arkansas has sought to prevent its teachers from discussing the theory of evolution because it is contrary to the belief of some that the Book of Genesis must be the exclusive source of doctrine as to the origin of man." It may be instead that the people's motive was merely that it would be best to remove this controversial subject from its schools; there is no reason I can imagine why a State is without power to withdraw from its curriculum any subject deemed too emotional and controversial for its public schools.

A . . . question that arises for me is whether this Court's decision forbidding a State to exclude the subject of evolution from its schools infringes the religious freedom of those who consider evolution an anti-religious doctrine. If the theory is considered anti-religious, as the Court indicates, how can the State be bound by the Federal Constitution to permit its teachers to advocate such an "anti-religious" doctrine to schoolchildren? . . . The Darwinian theory is said to challenge the Bible's story of creation; so too have some of those who believe in the Bible, along with many others, challenged the Darwinian theory. Since there is no indication that the literal Biblical doctrine of the origin of man is included in the curriculum of Arkansas schools, does not the removal of the subject of evolution leave the State in a neutral position toward these supposedly competing religious and anti-religious doctrines?

The Court, it seems to me, makes a serious mistake in bypassing the plain, unconstitutional vagueness of this statute in order to reach out and decide this troublesome, to me, First Amendment question. However wise this Court may be or may become hereafter, it is doubtful that, sitting in Washington, it can successfully supervise and censor the curriculum of every public school in every hamlet and city in the United States.

Mr. Justice STEWART, concurring in the result.

The States are most assuredly free "to choose their own curriculums for their own schools." A State is entirely free, for example, to decide that the only foreign language to be taught in its public school system shall be Spanish. But would a State be constitutionally free to punish a teacher for letting his students know that other languages are also spoken in the world? I think not.

It is one thing for a State to determine that "the subject of higher mathematics, or astronomy, or biology" shall or shall not be included in its public school curriculum. It is quite another thing for a State to make it a criminal offense for a public school teacher so much as to mention the very existence of an entire system of respected human thought. That kind of criminal law, I think, would clearly impinge upon the guarantees of free communication contained in the First Amendment, and made applicable to the States by the Fourteenth.

WISCONSIN v. YODER.

406 U. S. 205

Decided May 15, 1972 — one Justice dissenting.

Mr. Chief Justice BURGER delivered the opinion of the Court.

Respondents Jonas Yoder and Wallace Miller are members of the Old Order Amish religion, and respondent Adin Yutzy is a member of the Conservative Amish Mennonite Church. . . . Wisconsin's compulsory school-attendance law required them to cause their children to attend public or private school until reaching age 16 but the respondents declined to send their children, ages 14 and 15, to public school after they complete the eighth grade. The children were not enrolled in any private school, or within any recognized exception to the compulsory-attendance law, and they are conceded to be subject to the Wisconsin statute.

On complaint of the school district administrator for the public schools, respondents were charged, tried, and convicted of violating the compulsory-attendance law in Green County Court and were fined the sum of $5 each. Respondents defended on the ground that the application of the compulsory-attendance law violated their rights under the First and Fourteenth Amendments. The trial testimony showed that respondents beieved, in accordance with the tenets of Old Order Amish communities generally, that their children's attendance at high school, public or private, was contrary to the Amish religion and way of life. They believed that by sending their children to high school, they would not only expose themselves to the danger of the censure of the church community, but, as found by the county court, also endanger their own salvation and that of their children. The State stipulated that respondents' religious beliefs were sincere.

As a result of their common heritage, Old Order Amish communities today are characterized by a fundamental belief that salvation requires life in a church community separate and apart from the world and worldly influence. This concept of life aloof from the world and its values is central to their faith.

A related feature of Old Order Amish communities is their devotion to a life in harmony with nature and the soil . . . Amish beliefs require members of the community to make their living by farming or closely related activities. Broadly speaking, the Old Order Amish religion pervades and determines the entire mode of life of its adherents. . . . Adult baptism, which occurs in late adolescence, is the time at which Amish young people voluntarily undertake heavy obligations, not unlike the Bar Mitzvah of the Jews, to abide by the rules of the church community.

Amish objection to formal education beyond the eighth grade is firmly grounded in these central religious concepts. They object to the high school, and higher education generally, because the values they teach are in marked variance with Amish values and the Amish way of life; they view secondary school education as an impermissible exposure of their children to a "worldly" influence in conflict with their beliefs.

Formal high school education beyond the eighth grade is contrary to Amish beliefs, not only because it places Amish children in an environment hostile to Amish beliefs with increasing emphasis on competition in class work and sports and with pressure to conform to the styles, manners, and ways of the peer group, but also because it takes them away from their community, physically and emotionally, during the crucial and formative adolescent period of life. During this period, the children must acquire Amish attitudes favoring manual work and self-reliance and the specific skills needed to perform the adult role of an Amish farmer or housewife. . . . In short, high school attendance with teachers who are not of the Amish faith — and may even be hostile to it — interposes a serious barrier to the integration of the Amish child into the Amish religious community.

The Amish do not object to elementary education through the first eight grades as a general proposition because they agree that their children must have basic skills in the "three R's" in order to read the Bible, to be good farmers and citizens, and to be able to deal with non-Amish people when necessary in the course of daily affairs. They view such a basic education as acceptable because it does not significantly expose their children to worldly values or interfere with their development in the Amish community during the crucial adolescent period.

On the basis of such considerations, Dr. Hostetler [one of the experts on Amish society] testified that compulsory high school attendance could not only result in great psychological harm to Amish children, because of the conflicts it would produce, but would also, in his opinion, ultimately result in the destruction of the Old Order Amish church community as it exists in the United States today. The testimony of Dr. Donald A. Erickson, an expert witness on education, also showed that the Amish succeed in preparing their high school age children to be productive members of the Amish community.

Although the trial court in its careful findings determined that the Wisconsin compulsory school-attendance law "does interfere with the freedom of the Defendants to act in accordance with their sincere religious belief" it also concluded that the requirement of high school attendance until age 16 was a "reasonable and constitutional" exercise of governmental power, and therefore denied the motion to dismiss the charges. The Wisconsin Circuit Court affirmed the convictions. The Wisconsin Supreme Court, however, sustained respondents' claim under the Free Exercise Clause of the First Amendment and reversed the convictions.

There is no doubt as to the power of a State, having a high responsibility for education of its citizens, to impose reasonable regulations for the control and duration of basic education . . . . Yet even this paramount responsibility was, in *Pierce*, made to yield to the right of parents to provide an equivalent education in a privately operated system. . . . Thus, a State's interest in universal education, however highly we rank it, is not totally free from a balancing process when it impinges on fundamental rights and interests, such as those specifically protected by the Free Exercise Clause of the First Amendment, and the traditional interest of parents with respect to the religious upbringing of their children so long as they, in the words of *Pierce*, "prepare [them] for additional obligations."

The essence of all that has been said and written on the subject is that only those interests of the highest order and those not otherwise served can overbalance legitimate claims to the free exercise of religion. We can accept it as settled, therefore, that, however strong the State's interest in universal compulsory education, it is by no means absolute to the exclusion or subordination of all other interests.

We come then to the quality of the claims of the respondents concerning the alleged encroachment of Wisconsin's compulsory school-attendance statute on their rights and the rights of their children to the free exercise of the religious beliefs they and their forbears have adhered to for almost three centuries. . . . A way of life, however virtuous and admirable, may not be interposed as a barrier to reasonable state regulation of education if it is based on purely secular considerations; to have the protection of the Religion Clauses, the claims must be rooted in religious belief. Although a determination of what is a "religious" belief or practice entitled to constitutional protection may present a most delicate question, the very concept of ordered liberty precludes allowing every person to make his own standards on matters of conduct in which society as a whole has important interests.

Giving no weight to such secular considerations, however, we see that the record in this case abundantly supports the claim that the traditional way of life of the Amish is not merely a matter of personal preference, but one of deep religious conviction, shared by an organized group, and intimately related to daily living. . . . for the Old Order Amish, religion is not simply a matter of theocratic belief. As the expert witnesses explained, the Old Order Amish religion pervades and determines virtually their entire way of life, regulating it with the detail of the Talmudic diet through the strictly enforced rules of the church community.

So long as compulsory education laws were confined to eight grades of elementary basic education imparted in a nearby rural schoolhouse, with a large proportion of students of the Amish faith, the Old Order Amish had little basis to fear that school attendance would expose their children to the worldly influence they reject. But modern compulsory secondary education in rural areas is now largely carried on in a consolidated school, often remote from the student's home and alien to his daily home life. As the record so strongly shows, the values and programs of the modern secondary school are in sharp conflict with the fundamental mode of life mandated by the Amish religion . . . The conclusion is inescapable that secondary schooling, by exposing Amish children to worldly influences in terms of attitudes, goals, and values contrary to beliefs, and by substantially interfering with the religious development of the Amish child and his integration into the way of life of the Amish faith community at the crucial adolescent stage of development, contravenes the basic religious tenets and practice of the Amish faith, both as to the parent and the child.

In sum, the unchallenged testimony of acknowledged experts in education and religious history, almost 300 years of consistent practice, and strong evidence of a sustained faith pervading and regulating respondents' entire mode of life support the claim that enforcement of the State's requirement of compulsory formal education after the eighth grade would gravely endanger if not destroy the free exercise of respondents' religious beliefs.

Wisconsin concedes that under the Religion Clauses religious beliefs are absolutely free from the State's control, but it argues that "actions," even though religiously grounded, are outside the protection of the First Amendment. . . . It is true that activities of individuals, even when religiously based, are often subject to regulation by the States in the exercise of their undoubted power to promote the health, safety, and general welfare, or the Federal Government in the exercise of its deligated powers. . . . But to agree that religiously grounded conduct must often be subject to the broad police power of the State is not to deny that there are areas of conduct protected by the Free Exercise Clause of the First Amendment and thus beyond the power of the State to control, even under regulations of general applicability. . . . This case, therefore, does not become easier because respondents were convicted for their "actions" in refusing to send their children to the public high school; in this context belief and action cannot be neatly confined in logic-tight compartments.

Nor can this case be disposed of on the grounds that Wisconsin's requirement for school attendance to age 16 applies uniformly to all citizens of the State and does not, on its face, discriminate against religions or a particular religion, or that it is motivated by legitimate secular concerns. A regulation neutral on its face may, in its application, nonetheless offend the constitutional requirement for governmental neutrality if it unduly burdens the free exercise of religion.

The State advances two primary arguments in support of its system of compulsory education. It notes, as Thomas Jefferson pointed out early in our history, that some degree of education is necessary to prepare citizens to participate effectively and intelligently in our open political system if we are to preserve freedom and independence. Further, education prepares individuals to be self-reliant and self-sufficient participants in society. We accept these propositions.

However, the evidence adduced by the Amish in this case is persuasively to the effect that an additional one or two years of formal high school for Amish children in place of their long-established program of informal vocational education would do little to serve those interests. . . . It is one thing to say that compulsory education for a year to two beyond the eighth grade may be necessary when its goal is the preparation of the child for life in modern society as the majority live, but it is quite another if the goal of education be viewed as the preparation of the child for life in the separated agrarian community that is the keystone of the Amish faith.

No one can question the State's duty to protect children from ignorance but this argument does not square with the facts disclosed in the record. Whatever their idiosyncrasies as seen by the majority, this record strongly shows that the Amish community has been a highly successful social unit within our society, even if apart from the conventional "mainstream."

It is neither fair nor correct to suggest that the Amish are opposed to education beyond the eighth grade level. What this record shows is that they are opposed to conventional formal education of the type provided by a certified high school because it comes at the child's crucial adolescent period of religious development.

There can be no assumption that today's majority is "right" and the Amish and others like them are "wrong." A way of life that is odd or even erratic but interferes with no rights or interests of others is not to be condemned because it is different.

The State, however, supports its interest in providing an additional one or two years of compulsory high school education to Amish children because of the possibility that some such children will choose to leave the Amish community, and that if this occurs they will be ill-equipped for life. . . . There is no specific evidence of the loss of Amish adherents by attrition, nor is there any showing that upon leaving the Amish community Amish children, with their practical agricultural training and habits of industry and self-reliance, would become burdens on society because of educational shortcomings.

There is nothing in this record to suggest that the Amish qualities of reliability, self-reliance, and dedication to work would fail to find ready markets in today's society. Absent some contrary evidence supporting the State's position, we are unwilling to assume that persons possessing such valuable vocational skills and habits are doomed to become burdens to society should they determine to leave the Amish faith, nor is there any basis in the record to warrant finding that an additional one or two years of formal school education beyond the eighth grade would serve to eliminate any such problem that might exist.

The Amish alternative to formal secondary school education has enabled them to function effectively in their day-to-day life under self-imposed limitations on relations with the world, and to survive and prosper in contemporary society as a separate, sharply identifiable and highly self-sufficient community for more than 200 years in this country. In itself this is strong evidence that they are capable of fulfilling the social and political responsibilities of citizenship without compelled attendance beyond the eighth grade at the price of jeopardizing their free exercise of religious belief.

This case, of course, is not one in which any harm to the physical or mental health of the child or to the public safety, peace, order, or welfare has been demonstrated or may be properly inferred. The record is to the contrary, and any reliance on that theory would find no support in the evidence.

The State has at no point tried this case on the theory that respondents were preventing their children from attending school against their expressed desires, and indeed the record is to the contrary. The State's position from the outset has been that it is empowered to apply its compulsory-attendance law to Amish parents in the same manner as to other parents — that is, without regard to the wishes of the child. That is the claim we reject today.

The history and culture of Western civilization reflect a strong tradition of parental concern for the nurture and upbringing of their children. This primary role of the parents in the upbringing of their children is now established beyond debate as an enduring American tradition.

However read, the Court's holding in *Pierce* stands as a charter of the rights of parents to direct the religious upbringing of their children. And, when the interests of parenthood are combined with a free exercise claim of the nature revealed by this record, more than merely a "reasonable relation to some purpose within the competency of the State" is required to sustain the validity of the State's requirement under the First Amendment. To be sure, the power of the parent, even when linked to a free exercise claim, may be subject to limitation under *Prince* if it appears that parental decisions will jeopardize the health or safety of the child, or have a potential for significant social burdens. But in this case, the Amish have introduced persuasive evidence undermining the arguments the State has advanced to support its claims in terms of the welfare of the child and society as a whole.

For the reasons stated we hold, with the Supreme Court of Wisconsin, that the First and Fourteenth Amendments prevent the State from compelling respondents to cause their children to attend formal high school to age 16.

Aided by a history of three centuries as an identifiable religious sect and a long history as a successful and self-sufficient segment of American society, the Amish in his case have convincingly demonstrated the sincerity of their religious beliefs, the interrelationship of belief with their mode of life, the vital role that belief and daily conduct play in the continued survival of Old Order Amish communities and their religious organization, and the hazards presented by the State's enforcement of a statute generally valid as to others.

Nothing we hold is intended to undermine the general applicabibity of the State's compulsory school-attendance statutes or to limit the power of the State to promulgate reasonsble standards that, while not impairing the free exercise of religion, provide for continuing agricultural vocational education under parental and church guidance by the Old Order Amish or others similarly situated. The States have had a long history of amicable and effective relationships with church-sponsored schools, and there is no basis for assuming that, in this related context, reasonable standards cannot be established concerning the content of the continuing vocational education of Amish children under parental guidance, provided always that state regulations are not inconsistent with what we have said in this opinion.

CHAPTER II
THE STATE AND
SECTARIAN EDUCATION

Introduction

Extensive reference is made, in legal discussion, to precedent decisions. Anyone familiar with the history of litigation in this area of religion-state relations will recognize immediately the first decision to be presented in this chapter. Without hesitation, *Pierce v. Society of Sisters* may be classified as a precedent decision.

At bar in this decision, announced in 1925, was an Oregon statutory act requiring attendance by all normal children of the State between the ages of eight and sixteen years at the public schools of the State. Appellees were a private military school and a parochial school. It was the contention of the two schools that enforcement of the act would bring an end to the existence of the two schools. Moreover, enforcement of the act would unconstitutionally limit the right of the parents who desire the kind of education offered by the two institutions to freely elect such education.

It was the opinion of the Court, with no dissent, that the act in question "unreasonably interferes with the liberty of parents and guardians to direct the upbringing and education of children under their control." (268 U. S., at 534-535) While the state may regulate all schools within its borders, require certain standards of all teachers, and require that all children in that state attend schools, the state may not restrict or inhibit the right of parents to send their children to private or parochial schools which fulfill the legitimate requirements of the state. The so-called "Pierce doctrine" currently retains its status as the legal sanction for the existence of parochial and private schools as legitimate alternatives to public education.

The 1930 decision in *Cochran v. Louisiana State Board of Education* confronted the question of the propriety of state aid to both public and parochial school children. A major consideration in the decision, however, was the aid rendered to the students of parochial schools. At issue was a practice of the state which furnished textbooks, purchased with severance tax revenues, to all school children of the State, regardless of their attendance at public or nonpublic schools. Appellants, as taxpayers, challenged such use of tax moneys. Relying almost totally on the dicta of the Louisiana Supreme Court, the Supreme Court of the United States declared the practice to be in keeping with the Constitution. It was the conclusion of the Court that the practice had an intention and effect of benefiting the public in general and the child in particular. The practice did not provide aid and sustinance to the parochial schools of the State. This distinction between general aid to children and specific aid to institutions was to be an influential one in future decisions.

In 1947, the Court was again called upon to decide the constitutionality of legislation said to provide aid to the parochial schools. The issue in *Everson v. Board of Education* revolved about a New Jersey statute which authorized reimbursement to parents whose children attended parochial schools for the cost of transportation, by public carrier, of such children to the parochial schools. The appellant, as a taxpayer, charged that such use of tax moneys was in violation of the Constitution.

With four Justices dissenting, Mr. Justice Black, in delivering the opinion of the Court, admitted that this practice approached "the verge" of unconstitutional action. However, after a most thorough analysis of the First Amendment and its implications, it was the opinion of the Court that the New Jersey practice was not in violation of the Constitution. The state must be neutral with regard to religion; but it cannot be the adversary of religion. It was the judgment of the Court that to deny New Jersey the right to extend the benefits of public welfare legislation to all its citizens would create such an adversary relationship. This distinction between direct benefit to parochial schools and public welfare benefit to the students who attend such schools will be a pivotal distinction in future decisions.

The two dissenting opinions, in which four Justices joined, are reproduced in part. While too extensive for inclusion here, the dissenting opinion of Mr. Justice Rutledge (333 U. S., at 28) contains a detailed discussion of the history of the development of the First Amendment, a discussion which would be of considerable interest to some readers.

The decision in *Board of Education v. Allen* proved to be of significance for many later decisions. Under review was a New York statute requiring that textbooks approved for use in the public schools of the State be purchased by local school boards and that such textbooks be loaned, free of charge, to all children subject to the compulsory school attendance laws of the State in grades seven through twelve. Textbooks were to be loaned to public and private school students alike. Appellants held the statute to be in violation of the First Amendment.

Utilizing *Everson v. Board of Education*, 330 U. S. 1, Mr. Justice White, in delivering the opinion of the Court, held the practice to be legitimate under the provisions of the Constitution. Two crucial elements of the statute guided the opinion. First, the books were to be loaned to all students and thus the benefits of the statute extended to both public and nonpublic school students. Second, the books subject to loan under the terms of the statute were textbooks approved by the State for use in the public schools of the State. The Court found no evidence that books of a totally sectarian nature were provided under the statute.

Three Justices delivered dissenting opinions in *Allen*. The dissenting opinion of Mr. Justice Black, reproduced in part, illustrates the general line of objection of the three. Although not reproduced here, the dissenting opinion of Mr. Justice

Douglas, at 245, would be of interest to anyone concerned with the analysis of religious content in school textbooks.

In *Flast v. Cohen*, litigation centered upon the expenditure of funds through Titles I and II of the Elementary and Secondary Education Act of 1965. Although a legally complicated and technical decision, the ruling is nevertheless important for religion-state relations as it established standing for legal action by taxpayers in constitutional litigation. The crucial prior decision of the Supreme Court on taxpayer standing was *Frothingham v. Mellon*, 262 U. S. 447, in which the Court ruled "that a federal taxpayer is without standing to challenge the constitutionality of a federal statute." (392 U. S., at 85) In the present decision, the Court ruled that a federal taxpayer does have standing when constitutional questions are raised with regard to the collection and expenditure of tax moneys. While the decision does not speak directly to the disputed expenditure of funds under Titles I and II, it did settle this most important legal issue, thereby broadening the base of challenge with respect to the expenditure of tax moneys for sectarian purposes.

Title I of the Higher Education Facilities Act (1963) provided construction grants for buildings and facilities to institutions of higher education regardless of whether the recipient institution was public or private, sectarian or nonsectarian. The Act expressly excluded any facility or building to be used for religious purposes. The limitation upon the use of the building or facility was to be in force for a period of twenty years. This set of circumstances provoked the litigation in *Tilton v. Richardson*.

In announcing the judgment of the Court, Mr. Chief Justice Burger saw only one problem with the Act. The twenty-year time limit was seen to present constitutional problems as the building or facility could, after that period of time, be used to foster sectarian goals, thereby involving the state in religion. The time limit provision was seen to have no essential relationship to the total Act and, separated therefrom, was ruled unconstitutional. As so amended, the Act itself was held to be constitutional. Of particular interest is the systematic application of the tests developed by the Court in prior decisions for use in such litigation. Also of interest is the distinction drawn between church-related institutions of higher education and parochial elementary and secondary schools (403 U. S., at 685-686). An important prior ruling of the Court in this decision was *Walz v. Tax Comm'n*, 397 U. S. 664. Dissenting opinions to this decision are found at the end of the decision itself and at the end of *Lemon v. Kurtzman*.

June 28, 1971, was a significant day for litigation dealing with state aid to parochial schools or sectarian institutions of higher education. In *Tilton*, the Court rendered a decision concerning aid to sectarian institutions of higher education. In *Lemon v. Kurtzman*, a decision announced on the same day, statutes enacted in Pennsylvania and Rhode Island which provided for, among other things, salary supplements for teachers employed in parochial schools who taught only nonsectarian subjects were held to be unconstitutional. The important considerations were, first, the difference the Court perceived in *Tilton* between parochial elementary and secondary schools and sectarian institutions of higher education, and, second, the amount of state surveillance necessary to ensure the required separation of the secular from the sectarian in the parochial schools. This surveillance would require, at the parochial elementary and secondary level, a degree of involvement of the state in religious activity which, in the view of the Court, is disallowed by the First Amendment. Of importance in later decisions was the introduction of another "test" for such litigation — that of potential political divisiveness (403 U. S., at 622).

Dissenting and concurring opinions for both *Tilton* and *Lemon* are found at the end of this decision. The dissenting opinions are important due to the nature of the objections raised. Some problems discussed in these dissenting and concurring opinions have possible application to the question of teaching about religion in the public schools. Along with *Tilton*, the Court made extensive use of *Everson v. Board of Education*, 330 U. S. 1, *Board of Education v. Allen*, 392 U. S. 236, and *Walz v. Tax Comm'n*, 397 U. S. 664, in this decision.

While *Lemon v. Kurtzman* was in process of adjudication, contracts pursuant to the statute were drawn and money paid for services rendered in keeping with those contracts. In a second *Lemon v. Kurtzman*, suit was brought to challenge the payment of those funds inasmuch as the Court had ruled the statutes to be unconstitutional. In actuality, this decision delt more with the legal problem of retroactivity in noncriminal cases than with religion-state concerns and, thus, shed little light upon the religion-state relationship. The petition to force reimbursement of funds paid in keeping with the contracts drawn during litigation was denied with three Justices dissenting.

In *Levitt v. Committee for Public Education*, a New York statute provided for the reimbursement to nonpublic schools of costs incurred in the administration of mandated state testing programs. The Court held the statute to be unconstitutional. The decision turned on the view of the Court that it is impossible to separate the secular and the sectarian functions of the schools involved sufficiently to allow aid to the secular only. Of some potential importance in this decision was the rather absolute refusal of the Court to take seriously the argument that the State should assist sectarian schools in the provision of services mandated by the State.

The dispute at bar in *Hunt v. McNair* arose from a rather complicated act passed by the South Carolina legislature which allowed institutions of higher education to present plans for institutional expansion to State authority. If approved, bonds were to be issued by the State, the property and facilities conveyed to the State and loaned back to the college or university for use until the debt was paid. At that time, the facilities and property would be reconveyed to the institution of higher education.

The dispute was joined when a sectarian institution presented such a plan to the State for financing. Seeing no essential difference between this case and *Tilton*, 403 U. S. 672, the Court held the Act to be constitutional. The dissenting opinion, in which two Justices joined, was based upon the possibility of a high degree of state involvement in the affairs of the sectarian institution in the enforcement of the terms of the legislation.

Four closely related cases were considered in *Committee for Public Education v. Nyquist*, a ruling occasioned by New York legislation. This legislation called for three acts of assistance to nonpublic education: (1) provision of funds for the maintenance and repair of nonpublic school facilities and equipment; (2) a tuition reimbursement for parents of children who attended nonpublic schools and whose income levels indicated financial deprivation; and (3) a system of tax relief for those parents of children who attended nonpublic schools but who fail to qualify for the reimbursement provisions of number (2).

The three tests for First Amendment problems which the Court had evolved to that point — (1) the legislation must have a secular legislative purpose; (2) the legislation may neither advance nor inhibit religion; and (3) enactment of the legislation must avoid excessive governmental entanglement with religion (413 U. S., at 773) — were systematically applied to the statutes in question and each was found constitutionally wanting before such scrutiny. A fourth test was added to the group — the legislation must not bring about excessive political divisiveness (at 795). This test had been discussed in Lemon v. Kurtzman (403 U. S., at 622) and was here applied by Mr. Justice Powell in the opinion of the Court as another of the bench marks for such litigation.

The dissenting opinions are well-reasoned and important. Of particular significance in these dissenting opinions were two arguments. One held that the proposed tax credits to parents did not provide direct aid to sectarian schools and, therefore, were no more unconstitutional than were the provision of textbooks or bus transportation to students who attend sectarian schools. Secondly, it was held that the legislation at issue, in reality, provided assistance to the public schools in that such legislation would forstall the great financial strain which could be anticipated on the public sector if the students attending the parochial schools were forced, by reason of financial distress, to attend the public schools. Taken together, these dissenting opinions are excellent examples of the reasoning employed in seeking governmental aid for sectarian education.

On the day on which the decision in Nyquist was handed down, the decision in Sloan v. Lemon was also announced. The Sloan decision held a tuition reimbursement plan for parents whose children attended private nonsectarian and parochial schools, provided through a Pennsylvania statute, suffered from the same constitutional infirmaties as did the New York legislation ruled unconstitutional in Nyquist. The Pennsylvania statute was therefore held to be in violation of the Constitution.

In Sloan, Pennsylvania had attempted to correct the shortcomings of their earlier "Nonpublic Elementary and Secondary Education Act" held unconstitutional in Lemon v. Kurtaman, 403 U. S. 602. Mr. Justice Powell, in delivering the opinion of the Court on this second attempt, wrote firmly that constant attempts to provide such aid were not blocked by evolving doctrines of the Court, but by the restrictions of the First Amendment itself. The attempt to refine basically unconstitutional programs would be futile. The Court, however, was not of single mind. The dissenting opinions at 798 and 814 apply to both this ruling and to Nyquist.

Litigation in Wheeler v. Barrera focused on provisions of the Elementary and Secondary Education Act of 1965. According to the provisions of that Act, federal funds could be expended for special programs for educationally deprived children in both public and private schools.

Suit was brought charging that students in the private schools of the State of Missouri were not receiving the aid provided by the Act. Due to legal technicalities, the Court refused to rule on the issues presented. The discussion, nevertheless, does provide some indication of how the provision of such aid should be approached to avoid future litigation. In dissent, however, Mr. Justice Douglas wrote that the issue was not moot and that the Court should render a decision. It was his sense that evasion by the Court of the issues in question would not settle the matter and that future litigation could be expected.

Pennsylvania once again attempted to provide assistance to the parochial sector in that State and the issue was brought to the Supreme Court in *Meek v. Pittinger*. On this occasion, statutes had been enacted which provided auxiliary services, textbooks, and instructional material to the students of parochial schools and to the parochial schools themselves. Following *Allen*, 392 U.S. 236, the provision of textbooks was upheld, but following several other decisions, most notably *Committee for Public Education v. Nyquist*, 413 U.S. 756, the provision of teaching materials and equipment and the provision of auxiliary services — counseling, testing and psychological, and special education services — were held unconstitutional. Governmental entanglement and potential political divisiveness were the primary constitutional tests which the statutes in question failed to pass.

In his dissent, Mr. Justice Brennan argued that the textbook provision should be held unconstitutional in accordance with the political divisiveness test enunciated "without express recognition" in *Lemon I*, 403 U.S. 602. *Allen*, upon which the majority based its decision, was rendered prior to the enunciation of the fourth test, a test which should now be fatal to Pennsylvania's textbook provision statute. Two additional dissenting opinions agreed with the majority in upholding the textbook provision, but disagreed with the decision of unconstitutionality as applied to the other provisions of Pennsylvania's statute. The *Marburger* decision utilized by Mr. Justice Brennan in his dissent was a 1974 Memorandum Decision.

In *Roemer v. Board of Public Works*, the Supreme Court was asked to rule on a challenge brought against a Maryland statute which provided noncategorical grants to eligible sectarian colleges and universities. In announcing the judgment of the Court, Mr. Justice Blackmun systematically applied the four tests of *Lemon I* and found this statute to be unconstitutional. Again the distinction between parochial elementary and secondary education and sectarian higher education is clearly drawn. In the view of Mr. Justice Blackmun, the Court had now considered the relationship between the state and sectarian education at all levels from enough different approaches to clearly indicate the constitutional limitations which must be applied. The dissenting opinions, however, indicate some disagreement with Mr. Justice Blackmun's view. Along with *Lemon I*, important prior decisions of the Court used by the majority include *Tilton v. Richardson*, 403 U.S. 672, and *Hunt v. McNair*, 413 U.S. 734.

The most recent decision in this long history of litigation to be presented is the decision announced in *Wolman v. Walter*. In response to *Meek v. Pittinger*, Ohio enacted complex legislation in the attempt to provide constitutional assistance to the parochial schools of that State. In delivering the opinion of the Court, Mr. Justice Blackmun undertook specific analysis of each provision of the legislation. With three Justices dissenting, the Court held the provision of textbooks and the provision of standardized testing and scoring to be constitutional. With a single dissent, the Court also approved the provision of diagnostic services. Moreover, the Court approved, despite two dissenting Justices, the provision of therapeutic services. The Court ruled unconstitutional the provision of instructional materials and equipment and the provision of transportation for field trips, with three Justices dissenting in the ruling on the first provision, four dissenting in the latter. The key point in determining constitutionality of this complex legislation appeared to be the provision of general public welfare assistance which, at the same time, provided no direct contribution to the nonpublic schools themselves. The analysis undertaken by the Court should provide a valuable model for any future legislative attempts to provide aid for parochial schools. Important prior decisions of the Court utilized here included: *Everson v. Board of Education*, 330 U. S. 1; *Board of Education v. Allen*, 392 U. S. 236; *Levitt v. Committee for Public Education*, 413 U. S. 472; *Committee for Public Education v. Nyquist*, 413 U. S. 756; *Meek v. Pittinger*, 421 U. S. 349; and *Roemer v. Board of Public Works*, 426 U. S. 736. Three concurring and dissenting opinions are reproduced in part. Taken together, they illustrate the major objections to state aid to sectarian education among the Justices who remained unconvinced by the arguments of the majority.

PIERCE v. SOCIETY OF THE SISTERS OF THE HOLY NAMES OF JESUS AND MARY.

PIERCE v. HILL MILITARY ACADEMY.

268 U. S. 510

Decided June 1, 1925.

Mr. Justice McREYNOLDS delivered the opinion of the Court.

The challenged act, effective September 1, 1926, requires every parent, guardian, or other person having control or charge or custody of a child between 8 and 16 years to send him "to a public school for the period of time a public school shall be held during the current year" in the district where the child resides; and failure so to do is declared a misdemeanor. There are exemptions — not specially important here . . . The manifest purpose is to compel general attendance at public schools by normal children, between 8 and 16, who have not completed the eighth grade. And without doubt enforcement of the statute would seriously impair, perhaps destroy, the profitable features of appelles' business and greatly diminish the value of their property.

Appellee the Society of Sisters is an Oregon corporation, organized in 1880, with power to care for orphans, educate and instruct the youth, establish and maintain academies or schools, and acquire necessary real and personal property. . . . In its primary schools many children between those ages are taught the subjects usually pursued in Oregon public schools during the first eight years. Systematic religious instruction and moral training according to the tenets of the Roman Catholic Church are also regularly provided.

After setting out the above facts, the Society's bill alleges that the enactment conflicts with the right of parents to choose schools where their children will receive appropriate mental and religious training, the right of the child to influence the parents' choice of a school, the right of schools and teachers therein to engage in a useful business or profession, and is accordingly repugnant to the Constitution and void. And, further, that unless enforcement of the measure is enjoined the corporation's business and property will suffer irreparable injury.

Appellee Hill Military Academy is a private corporation organized in 1908 under the laws of Oregon, engaged in owning, operating, and conducting for profit an elementary, college preparatory, and military training school for boys between the ages of 5 and 21 years. . . . the courses of study conform to the requirements of the state board of education. . . . By reason of the statute and threat of enforcement appellee's business is being destroyed and its property depriciated; parents and guardians are refusing to make contracts for the future instruction of their sons, and some are being withdrawn.

No question is raised concerning the power of the state reasonably to regulate all schools, to inspect, supervise and examine them, their teachers and pupils; to require that all children of proper age attend some school, that treachers shall be of good moral character and patriotic disposition, that certain studies plainly essential to good citizenship must be taught, and that nothing be taught which is manifestly inimical to the public welfare.

The inevitable practical result of enforcing the act under consideration would be destruction of appellees' primary schools, and perhaps all other private primary schools for normal children within the state of Oregon. Appellees are engaged in a kind of undertaking not inherently harmful, but long regarded as useful and meritorious.

. . . we think it entirely plain that the Act of 1922 unreasonably interferes with the liberty of parents and guardians to direct the upbringing and education of children under their control. As often heretofore pointed out, rights guaranteed by the Constitution may not be abridged by legislation which has no reasonable relation to some purpose within the competency of the state. The fundamental theory of liberty upon which all governments in this Union repose excludes any general power of the state to standardize its children by forcing them to accept instruction from public teachers only. The child is not the mere creature of the state; those who nurture him and direct his destiny have the right, coupled with the high duty, to recognize and prepare him for additional obligations.

Generally, it is entirely true, as urged by counsel, that no person in any business has such an interest in possible customers as to enable him to restrain exercise of proper power of the state upon the ground that he will be deprived of patronage. But the injunctions here sought are not against the exercise of any proper power. Appellees asked protection against arbitrary, unreasonable, and unlawful interference with their partons and the consequent destruction of their business and property. Their interest is clear and immediate . . .

COCHRAN v. LOUISIANA STATE BOARD OF EDUCATION.

281 U. S. 370

Decided April 28, 1930.

Mr. Chief Justice HUGHES delivered the opinion of the Court.

The appellants, as citizens and taxpayers of the state of Louisiana, brought this suit to restrain the State Board of Education and other state officials from expending any part of the severance tax fund in purchasing school books and in supplying them free of cost to the school children of the state ... upon the ground that the legislation violated specified provisions of the Constitution of the state and also section 4 of article 4 and the Fourteenth Amendment of the Federal Constitution.

No substantial Federal question is presented under section 4 of article 4 of the Federal Constitution . . .

The contention of the appellant under the Fourteenth Amendment is that taxation for the purchase of school books constituted a taking of private property for a private purpose. . . . The purpose is said to be to aid private, religious, sectarian, and other schools not embraced in the public educational system of the state by furnishing text-books free to the children attending such private schools. The operation and effect of the legislation in question were described by the Supreme Court of the state as follows . . . "One may scan the acts in vain to ascertain where any money is appropriated for the purchase of school books for the use of any church, private, sectarian, or even public school. The appropriations were made for the specific purpose of purchasing school books for the use of the school children of the state, free of cost to them. It was for their benefit and the resulting benefit to the state that the appropriations were made. True, these children attend some school, public or private, the latter, sectarian or nonsectarian, and that the books are to be furnished them for their use, free of cost, whichever they attend. The schools, however, are not the beneficiaries of these appropriations. . . . It is also true that the sectarian schools, which some of the children attend, instruct their pupils in religion, and books are used for that purpose, but one may search diligently the acts, though without result, in an effort to find anything to the effect that it is the purpose of the state to furnish religious books for the use of such children. . . . What the statutes contemplate is that the same books that are furnished children attending public schools shall be furnished children attending private schools. This is the only practical way of interpreting and executing the statutes, and this is what the state board of education is doing. . . ."

Viewing the statute as having the effect thus attributed to it, we cannot doubt that the taxing power of the state is exerted for a public purpose. The legislation does not segregate private schools, or their pupils, as its beneficiaries or attempt to interfere with any matters of exclusively private concern. Its interest is education, broadly; its method, comprehensive. Individual interests are aided only as the common interest is safeguarded.

EVERSON v. BOARD OF EDUCATION OF EWING TP.

330 U. S. 1

Decided February 10, 1947 — four Justices dissenting.

Mr. Justice BLACK delivered the opinion of the Court.

A New Jersey statute authorizes its local school districts to make rules and contracts for the transportation of children to and from schools. The appellee, a township board of education, acting pursuant to this statute authorized reimbursement to parents of money expended by them for the bus transportation of their children on regular busses operated by the public transportation system. Part of this money was for the payment of transportation of some children in the community to Catholic parochial schools.

The appellant, in his capacity as a district taxpayer, filed suit in a State court challenging the right of the Board to reimburse parents of parochial school students.

Since there has been no attack on the statute on the ground that a part of its language excludes children attending private schools operated for profit from enjoying state payment for their transportation, we need not consider this exclusionary language; it has no relevancy to any constitutional question here presented. . . . Consequently, we put to one side the question as to the validity of the statute against the claim that it does not authoirize payment for the transportation generally of school children in New Jersey.

The only contention here is that the State statute and the resolution, in so far as they authorize reimbursement to parents of children attending parochial schools, violate the Federal Constitution in these two respects, which to some extent, overlap. First. They authorize the State to take by taxation the private property of some and bestow it upon others, to be used for their own private purposes. This, it is alleged violates the due process clause of the Fourteenth Amendment. Second. The statute and the resolution forced inhabitants to pay taxes to help support and maintain schools which are dedicated to, and which regularly teach, the Catholic Faith. This is alleged to be a use of State power to support church schools contrary to the prohibition of the First Amendment which the Fourteenth Amendment made applicable to the states.

First. The due process argument that the State law taxes some people to help others carry on their private purposes is framed in two phases. The first phase is that a state cannot tax A to reimburse B for the cost of transporting his children to church schools. . . . the New Jersey legislature has decided that a public purpose will be served by using tax-raised funds to pay the bus fares of all school children, including those who attend parochial schools. . . . The fact that a state law, passed to sastify a public need, coincides with the personal desires of the individuals most directly affected is certainly an inadequate reason for us to say that a legislature has erroneously appraised the public need.

Insofar as the second phase of the due process argument may differ from the first, it is by suggesting that taxation for transportation of children to church schools constitutes support of a religion by the State. But if the law is invalid for this reason, it is because it violates the First Amendment's prohibition against the establishment of religion by law. This is the exact question raised by appellant's second contention, to consideration of which we now turn.

Second. The New Jersey statute is challenged as a "law respecting an establishment of religion.". . . These words of the First Amendment reflected in the minds of early Americans a vivid mental picture of conditions and practices which they fervently wished to stamp out in order to preserve liberty for themselves and for their posterity. Doubtless their goal has not been entirely reached; but so far has the Nation moved toward it that the expression "law respecting an establishment of religion," probably does not so vividly remind present-day Americans of the evils, fears, and political problems that caused that expression to be written into our Bill of Rights. Whether this New Jersey law is one respecting the "establishment of religion" requires an understanding of the meaning of that language, particularly with respect to the imposition of taxes.

A large proportion of the early settlers of this country came here from Europe to escape the bondage of laws which compelled them to support and attend government favored churches. . . . In efforts to force loyalty to whatever religious group happened to be on top and in league with the government of a particular time and place, men and women had been fined, cast in jail, cruelly tortured, and killed.

These practices of the old world were transplanted to and began to thrive in the soil of the new America. The very charters granted by the English Crown to the individuals and companies designated to make the laws which would control the destinies of the colonials authorized these individuals and companies to erect religious establishments which all, whether believers or non-believers, would be required to support and attend. . . . And all . . . dissenters were compelled to pay tithes and taxes to support government-sponsored churches whose ministers preached inflamatory sermons designed to strengthen and consolidate the established faith by generating a burning hatred against dissenters.

These practices became so commonplace as to shock the freedom-loving colonials into a feeling of abhorrence. The imposition of taxes to pay ministers' salaries and to build and maintain churches and church property aroused their indignation. It was these feelings which found expression in the First Amendment. No one locality and no one group throughout the Colonies can rightly be given entire credit for having aroused the sentiment that culminated in adoption of the Bill of Rights' provisions embracing religious liberty. But Virginia, where the established church had achieved a dominant influence in political affairs and where many excesses attracted wide public attention, provided a great stimulus and able leadership for the movement.

The movement ... reached its dramatic climax in Virginia in 1785-86 when the Virginia legislative body was about to renew Virginia's tax levy for the support of the established church. Thomas Jefferson and James Madison led the fight against this tax. Madison wrote his great Memorial and Remonstrance against the law. In it, he eloquently argued that a true religion did not need the support of law; that no person, either believer or non-believer, should be taxed to support a religious institution of any kind; that the best interest of a society required that the minds of men always be wholly free; and that cruel persecutions were the inevitable result of government-established religions. Madison's Remonstrance received strong support throughout Virginia, and the Assembly postponed consideration of the proposed tax measure until its next session. When the proposal came up for consideration at that session, it not only died in committee, but the Assembly enacted the famous "Virginia Bill for Religious Liberty" originally written by Thomas Jefferson.

This Court has previously recognized that the provisions of the First Amendment, in the drafting and adoption of which Madison and Jefferson played such leading roles, had the same objective and were intended to provide the same protection against governmental intrusion on religious liberty as the Virginia statute. ... In recent years ... the question has most frequently arisen in connection with proposed state aid to church schools and efforts to carry on religious teachings in the public schools in accordance with the tenets of a particular sect. ... The state courts, in the main, have remained faithful to the language of their own constitutional provisions designed to protect religious freedom and to separate religions and governments. Their decisions, however, show the difficulty in drawing the line between tax legislation which provides funds for the welfare of the general public and that which is designed to support institutions which teach religion.

The broad meaning given the Amendment by ... earlier cases has been accepted by this Court in its decisions concerning an individual's religious freedom rendered since the Fourteenth Amendment was interpreted to make the prohibitions of the First applicable to state action abridging religious freedom. There is every reason to give the same application and broad interpretation to the "establishment of religion" clause.

The "establishment of religion" clause of the First Amendment means at least this: Neither a state nor the Federal Government can set up a church. Neither can pass laws which aid one religion, aid all religions, or prefer one religion over another. Niether can force nor influence a person to go to or to remain away from church against his will or force him to profess a belief or disbelief in any religion. No person can be punished for entertaining or professing religious beliefs or disbeliefs, for church attendance or non-attendance. No tax in any amount, large or small, can be levied to support any religious activities or institutions, whatever they many be called, or whatever form they may adopt to teach or practice religion. Neither a state nor the Federal Government can, openly or secretly, participate in the affairs of any religious organizations or groups and vice versa. In the words of Jefferson, the clause against establishment of religion by law was intended to erect "a wall of separation between Church and State."

We must consider the New Jersey statute in accordance with the foregoing limitations imposed by the First Amendment. But we must not strike that state statute down if it is within the state's constitutional power even though it approaches the verge of that power. . . . New Jersey cannot consistently with the "establishment of religion" clause of the First Amendment contribute tax-raised funds to the support of an institution which teaches the tenets and faith of any church. On the other hand, other language of the amendment commands that New Jersey cannot hamper its citizens in the free exercise of their own religion. Consequently, it cannot exclude individual Catholics, Lutherans, Mohammedans, Baptists, Jews, Methodists, Non-believers, Presbyterians, or the members of any other faith, *because of their faith, or lack of it,* from receiving the benefits of public welfare legislation. While we do not mean to intimate that a state could not provide transportation only to children attending public schools, we must be careful, in protecting the citizens of New Jersey against state-established churches, to be sure that we do not inadvertently prohibit New Jersey from extending its general State law benefits to all its citizens without regard to their religious belief.

Measured by these standards, we cannot say that the First Amendment prohibits New Jersey from spending tax-raised funds to pay the bus fares of parochial school pupils as a part of a general program under which it pays the fares of pupils attending public and other schools. . . . the First Amendment . . . requires the state to be a neutral in its relations with groups of religious believers and non-believers; it does not require the state to be their adversary. State power is no more to be used so as to handicap religions, than it is to favor them.

This Court has said that parents may, in the discharge of their duty under state compulsory education laws, send their children to a religious rather than a public school if the school meets the secular educational requirements which the state has power to impose. . . . It appears that these parochial schools meet New Jersey's requirements. The State contributes no money to the schools. It does not support them. Its legislation, as applied, does no more than provide a general program to help parents get their children, regardless of their religion, safely and expeditiously to and from accredited schools.

The First Amendment has erected a wall between church and state. That wall must be kept high and impregnable. We could not approve the slightest breach. New Jersey has not breached it here.

Mr. Justice JACKSON, dissenting.

The Court's opinion marshals every argument in favor of state aid and puts the case in its most favorable light, but much of its reasoning confirms my conclusions that there are no good grounds upon which to support the present legislation. In fact, the undertones of the opinion, advocating complete and uncompromising separation of Church and State, seem utterly discordant with its conclusion yielding support to their commingling in educational matters.

The New Jersey Act in question makes the character of the school, not the needs of the children determine the eligibility of parents to reimbursement. The Act permits payment for transportation to parochial schools or public schools but prohibits it to private schools operated in whole or in part for profit.

If we are to decide this case on the facts before us, our question is simply this: Is it constitutional to tax this complainant to pay the cost of carrying pupils to Chruch schools of one specified denomination?

The Constitution says nothing of education. It lays no obligation on the states to provide schools and does not undertake to regulate state systems of education if they see fit to maintain them. But they cannot, through school policy any more than through other means, invade rights secured to citizens by the Constitution of the United States.

The Roman Catholic Church, counseled by experience in many ages and many lands and with all sorts and conditions of men, takes what, from the viewpoint of its own progress and the success of its mission, is a wise estimate of the importance of education to religion. It does not leave the individual to pick up religion by chance.

Our public school, if not a product of Protestantism, at least is more consistent with it than with the Catholic culture and scheme of values. It is a relatively recent development dating from about 1840. It is organized on the premise that secular education can be isolated from all religious teaching so that the school can inculcate all needed temporal knowledge and also maintain a strict and lofty neutrality as to religion. The assumption is that after the individual has been instructed in worldly wisdom he will be better fitted to choose his religion.

It is of no importance in this situation whether the beneficiary of this expenditure of tax-raised funds is primarily the parochial school and incidentally the pupil, or whether the aid is directly bestowed on the pupil with indirect benefits to the school. The state cannot maintain a Church and it can no more tax its citizens to furnish free carriage to those who attend a Church.

. . . the religious freedom Amendment to our Constitution was to take every form of propagation of religion out of the realm of things which could directly or indirectly be made public business and thereby be supported in whole or in part at taxpayers' expense. That is a difference which the Constitution sets up between religion and almost every other subject matter of legislation, a difference which goes to the very root of religious freedom and which the Court is overlooking today.

Mr. Justice RUTLEDGE, with whom Mr. Justice FRANKFURTER, Mr. Justice JACKSON and Mr. Justice BURTON agree, dissenting.

This case forces us to determine squarely for the first time what was "an establishment of religion" in the First Amendment's conception . . .

Not simply an established church, but any law respecting an establishment of religion is forbidden. The Amendment was broadly but not loosely phrased.

The Amendment's purpose was not to strike merely at the official establishment of a single sect, creed or religion, outlawing only a formal relation such as had prevailed in England and some of the colonies. Necessarily it was to uproot all such relationships. But the object was broader than separating church and state in this narrow sense. It was to create a complete and permanent separation of the spheres of religious activity and civil authority by comprehensively forbidding every form of public aid or support for religion.

"Religion" appears only once in the Amendment. But the word governs two prohibitions and governs them alike. It does not have two meanings, one narrow to forbid "an establishment" and another, much broader, for securing "the free exercise thereof."

. . . the Amendment . . . secures all forms of religious expression, credal, sectarian or nonsectarian wherever and however taking place, except conduct which trenches upon the like freedoms of others or clearly and presently endangers the community's good order and security.

"Religion" has the same broad significance in the twin prohibition concerning "an establishment." The Amendment was not duplicitous. "Religion" and "establishment" were not used in any formal or technical sense. The prohibition broadly forbids state support, financial or other, of religion in any guise, form or degree. It outlaws all use of public funds for religious purposes.

In the documents of the times, particularly of Madison, who was leader in the Virginia struggle before he became the Amendment's sponsor, but also in the writings of Jefferson and others and in the issues which engendered them is to be found irrefutable confirmation of the Amendment's sweeping content.

For Madison, as also for Jefferson, religious freedom was the crux of the struggle for freedom in general.

As the Remonstrance discloses throughout, Madison opposed every form and degree of official relation between religion and civil authority. For him religion was a wholly private matter beyond the scope of civil power either to restrain or to support. . . . "Establishment" and "free exercise" were correlative and coextensive ideas, representing only different facets of the single great and fundamental freedom.

In no phase was he more unrelentingly absolute than in opposing state support or aid by taxation. . . . Madison and his coworkers made no exceptions or abridgements to the complete separation they created. Their objection was not to small tithes. It was to any tithes whatsoever.

In view of this history no further proof is needed that the Amendment forbids any appropriation, large or small, from public funds to aid or support any and all religious exercises. But if more were called for, the debates in the First Congress and this Court's consistent expressions, whenever it has touched on the matter directly, supply it.

Compulsory attendance upon religious exercises went out early in the process of separating church and state, together with forced observance of religious forms and ceremonies. Test oaths and religious qualification for office followed later. These things none devoted to our great tradition of religious liberty would think of bringing back. Hence today, apart from efforts to inject religious training or exercises and sectarian issues into the public schools, the only serious surviving threat to maintaining that complete and permanent separation of religion and civil power which the First Amendment commands is through use of the taxing power to support religion, religious establishments, or establishments having a religious foundation whatever their form or special religious function.

Does New Jersey's action furnish support for religion by use of the taxing power? Certainly it does, if the test remains undiluted as Jefferson and Madison made it, that money taken by taxation from one is not to be used or given to support another's religious training or belief, or indeed one's own.

The funds used here were raised by taxation. The Court does not dispute nor could it that their use does in fact give aid and encouragement to religious instruction. It only concludes that this aid is not "support" in law.... Here parents pay money to send their children to parochial schools and funds raised by taxation are used to reimburse them. This not only helps the children to get to school and the parents to send them. It aids them in a substantial way to get the very thing which they are sent to the particular school to secure, namely, religious training and teaching.

It is precisely because the instruction is religious and relates to a particular faith, whether one or another, that parents send their children to religious schools under the Pierce doctrine. And the very purpose of the state's contribution is to defray the cost of conveying the pupil to the place where he will receive not simply secular, but also and primarily reigious, teaching and guidance.

Without buildings, without equipment, without library, textbooks and other materials, and without transportation to bring teacher and pupil together in such an effective teaching environment, there can be not even the skeleton of what our times require. Hardly can it be maintained that transportation is the least essential of these items ...

No one conscious of religious values can be unsympathetic toward the burden which our constitutional separation puts on parents who desire religious instruction mixed with secular for their children. They pay taxes for others' children's education, at the same time the added cost of instruction for their own.

But if those feelings should prevail, there would be an end to our historic constitutional policy and command. No more unjust or discriminatory in fact is it to deny attendants at religious schools the cost of their transportation than it is to deny them tuitions, sustenance for their teachers, or any other educational expense which others receive at public cost.

Of course discrimination in the legal sense does not exist. The child attending the religious school has the same right as any other to attend the public school. But he foregoes exercising it because the same guaranty which assures this freedom forbids the public school or any agency of the state to give or aid him in securing the religious instruction he seeks.

Were he to accept the common school, he would be the first to protest the teaching there of any creed or faith not his own. And it is precisely for the reason that their atmosphere is wholly secular that children are not sent to public schools under the Pierce doctrine. But that is a constitutional necessity, because we have staked the very existence of our country on the faith that complete separation between the state and religion is best for the state and best for religion.

That policy necessarily entails hardship upon persons who forego the right to educational advantages the state can supply in order to secure others it is precluded from giving.... But it does not make the state unneutral to withhold what the Constitution forbids it to give. On the contrary it is only by observing the prohibition rigidly that the state can maintain its neutrality and avoid partisanship in the dissensions inevitable when sect opposes sect over demands for public moneys to further religious education, teaching or training in any form or degree, directly or indirectly.

Two great drives are constantly in motion to abridge, in the name of education, the complete division of religion and civil authority which our forefathers made. One is to introduce religious education and observances into the public schools. The other, to obtain public funds for the aid and support of various private religious schools.... In my opinion both avenues were closed by the Constitution. Neither should be opened by this Court.

BOARD OF EDUCATION OF CENTRAL SCHOOL DISTRICT NO.1 v. ALLEN

392 U. S. 236

Decided June 10, 1968 — three Justices dissenting.

Mr. Justice WHITE delivered the opinion of the Court.

A law of the State of New York requires local public school authorities to lend textbooks free of charge to all students in grades seven through 12; students attending private schools are included. This case presents the question whether this statute is a "law respecting an establishment of religion, or prohibiting the free exercise thereof," and so in conflict with the First and Fourteenth Amendments to the Constitution, because it authorizes the loan of textbooks to students attending parochial schools. We hold that the law is not in violation of the Constitution.

Until 1965, § 701 of the Education Law of the State of New York ... authorized public school boards to designate textbooks for use in the public schools, to purchase such books with public funds, and to rent or sell the books to public school students. ... Beginning with the 1966-1967 school year, local school boards were required to purchase textbooks and lend them without charge "to all children residing in such district who are enrolled in grades seven to twelve of a public or private school which complies with the compulsory education law." The books now loaned are "text-books which are designed for use in any public, elementary or secondary schools of the state or are approved by any boards of education," and which — according to a 1966 amendment — "a pupil is required to use as a text for a semester or more in a particular class in the school he legally attends."

Everson v. Board of Education, 330 U. S. 1 (1947), is the case decided by this Court that is most nearly in point for today's problem.... The Court stated that the Establishment Clause bars a State from passing "laws which aid one religion, aid all religions, or prefer one religion over another," and bars too any "tax in any amount, large or small ... levied to support any religious activities or institutions .. ." Nevertheless, said the Court, the Establishment Clause does not prevent a State from extending the benefits of state laws to all citizens without regard for their religious affiliation and does not prohibit "New Jersey from spending tax-raised funds to pay the bus fares of parochial school pupils as a part of a general program under which it pays the fares of pupils attending public and other schools."

Everson and later cases have shown that the line between state neutrality to religion and state support of religion is not easy to locate. "The constitutional standard is the separation of Church and State. The problem, like many problems in constitutional law, is one of degree."

The statute upheld in *Everson* would be considered a law having "a secular legislative purpose and a primary effect that neither advances nor inhibits religion." We reach the same result with respect to the New York law requiring school books to be loaned free of charge to all students in specified grades. . . . The law merely makes available to all children the benefits of a general program to lend school books free of charge. Books are furnished at the request of the pupil and ownership remains, at least technically, in the State. Thus no funds or books are furnished to parochial schools, and the financial benefit is to parents and children, not to schools. Perhaps free books make it more likely that some children choose to attend a sectarian school, but that was true of the state-paid bus fares in *Everson* and does not alone demonstrate an unconstitutional degree of support for a religious institution.

Of course books are different from buses. Most bus rides have no inherent religious significance, while religious books are common. However, the language of § 701 does not authorize the loan of religious books . . . Although the books loaned are those required by the parochial school for use in specific courses, each book loaned must be approved by the public school authorities; only secular books may receive approval. . . . In judging the validity of the statute on this record we must proceed on the assumption that books loaned to students are books that are not unsuitable for use in the public schools because of religious content.

The major reason offered by appellants for distinguishing free textbooks from free bus fares is that books, but not buses, are critical to the teaching process, and in a sectarian school that process is employed to teach religion. However this Court has long recognized that religious schools pursue two goals, religious instruction and secular education. In the leading case of *Pierce v. Society of Sisters*, 268 U. S. 510 (1925), the Court held that although it would not question Oregon's power to compel school attendance or require that the attendance be at an institution meeting State-imposed requirements as to quality and nature of curriculum, Oregon had not shown that its interest in secular education required that all children attend publicly operated schools. A premise of this holding was the view that the State's interest in education would be served sufficiently by reliance on the secular teaching that accompanied religious training in the schools maintained by the Society of Sisters.

Americans care about the quality of the secular education available to their children. They have considered high quality education to be an indispensable ingredient for achieving the kind of nation, and the kind of citizenry, that they have desired to create. Considering this attitude, the continued willingness to rely on private school systems, including parochial systems, strongly suggests that a wide segment of informed opinion, legislative and otherwise, has found that those schools do an acceptable job of providing secular education to their students. This judgment is further evidence that parochial schools are performing, in addition to their sectarian function, the task of secular education.

Nothing in this record supports the proposition that all textbooks, whether they deal with mathematics, physics, foreign languages, history, or literature, are used by the parochial schools to teach religion.... We are unable to hold, based solely on judicial notice, that this statute results in unconstitutional involvement of the State with religious instruction or that § 701, for this or the other reasons urged, is a law respecting the establishment of religion within the meaning of the First Amendment.

Mr. Justice BLACK, dissenting.

The *Everson* and *McCollum* cases plainly interpret the First and Fourteenth Amendments as protecting the taxpayers of a State from being compelled to pay taxes to their government to support the agencies of private religious organizations the taxpayers oppose. To authorize a State to tax its residents for such church purposes is to put the State squarely in the religious activities of certain religious groups that happen to be strong enough politically to write their own religious preferences and prejudices into the laws. This links state and churches together in controlling the lives and destinies of our citizenship — a citizenship composed of people of myriad religious faiths, some of them bitterly hostile to and completely intolerant of the others.

It is true, of course, that the New York law does not as yet formally adopt or establish a state religion. But it takes a great stride in that direction and coming events cast their shadows before them. The same powerful sectarian religious propagandists who have succeeded in securing passage of the present law to help religious schools carry on their sectarian religious purposes can and doubtless will continue their propaganda, looking toward complete domination and supremacy of their particular brand of religion. And it nearly always is by insidious approaches that the citadels of liberty are most successfully attacked.

I know of no prior opinion of this Court upon whch the majority here can rightfully rely to support its holding this New York law constitutional.

As my Brother DOUGLAS so forcefully shows, in an argument with which I fully agree, upholding a State's power to pay bus or streetcar fares for school children cannot provide support for the validity of a state law using tax-raised funds to buy books for a religious school. The First Amendment's bar to establishment of religion must preclude a State from using funds levied from all of its citizens to purchase books for use by sectarian schools, which, although "secular," realistically will in some way inevitably tend to propagate the religious views of the favored sect. Books are the most essential tool of education since they contain the resources of knowledge which the educational process is designed to exploit. In this sense it is not difficult to distinguish books, which are the heart of any school, from bus fares, which provide a convenient and helpful general public transportation service. With respect to the former, state financial support actively and directly assists the teaching and propagation of sectarian religious viewpoints in clear conflict with the First Amendment's establishment bar; with respect to the latter, the State merely provides a general and nondiscriminatory transportation service in no way related to substantive religious views and beliefs.

FLAST v. COHEN.

392 U. S. 83

Decided June 10, 1968 — one Justice dissenting.

Mr. Chief Justice WARREN delivered the opinion of the Court.

In *Frothingham v. Mellon*, 262 U. S. 447 (1923), this Court ruled that a federal taxpayer is without standing to challenge the constitutionality of a federal statute. That ruling has stood for 45 years as an impenetrable barrier to suits against Acts of Congress brought by individuals who can assert only the interest of federal taxpayers. In this case, we must decide whether the *Frothingham* barrier should be lowered when a taxpayer attacks a federal statute on the ground that it violates the Establishment and Free Exercise Clauses of the First Amendment.

While disclaiming any intent to challenge as unconstitutional all programs under Title I of the Act, the complaint alleges that federal funds have been disbursed under the Act, "with the consent and approval of the [appellees]," and that such funds have been used and will continue to be used to finance "instruction in reading, arithmetic and other subjects and for guidance in religious and sectarian schools" and "the purchase of textbooks and instructional and library materials for use in religious and sectarian schools." Such expenditures of federal tax funds, appellants alleged, violate the First Amendment because "they constitute a law respecting an establishment of religion" and because "they prohibit the free exercise of religion on the part of the [appellants] . . . by reason of the fact that they constitute compulsory taxation for religious purposes."

This Court first faced squarely the question whether a litigant asserting only his status as a taxpayer has standing to maintain a suit in a federal court in *Forthingham v. Mellon* . . . and that decision must be the starting point for analysis in this case. The taxpayer in *Frothingham* attacked as unconstitutional the Maternity Act of 1921 . . . which established a federal program of grants to those States which would undertake programs to reduce maternal and infant mortality. . . . the Court ruled that the taxpayer had failed to allege the type of "direct injury" necessary to confer standing.

Although the barrier *Frothingham* erected against federal taxpayer suits has never been breached, the decision has been the source of some confusion and the object of considerable criticism. The confusion has developed as commentators have tried to determine whether *Frothingham* establishes a constitutional bar to taxpayer suits or whether the Court was simply imposing a rule of self-restraint which was not constitutionally compelled.

. . . we find no absolute bar in Article III to suits by federal taxpayers challenging allegedly unconstitutional federal taxing and spending programs. There remains, however, the problem of determining the circumstances under which a federal taxpayer will be deemed to have the personal stake and interest that impart the necessary concrete adverseness to such litigation so that standing can be conferred on the taxpayer *qua* taxpayer consistent with the constitutional limitations of Article III.

The nexus demanded of federal taxpayers has two aspects to it. First, the taxpayer must establish a logical link between that status and the type of legislative enactment attacked. Thus, a taxpayer will be a proper party to allege the unconstitutionality only of exercises of congressional power under the taxing and spending clause of Art. I, § 8, of the Constitution. . . . Secondly, the taxpayer must establish a nexus between that status and the precise nature of the constitutional infringement alleged. Under this requirement, the taxpayer must show that the challenged enactment exceeds specific constitutional limitations imposed upon the exercise of the congressional taxing and spending power and not simply that the enactment is generally beyond the powers deligated to Congress by Art. I, § 8. When both nexuses are established, the litigant will have shown a taxpayer's stake in the outcome of the controversy and will be a proper and appropriate party to invoke a federal court's jurisdiction.

The taxpayer-appellants in this case have satisfied both nexuses to support their claim of standing under the test we announce today.

We have noted that the Establishment Clause of the First Amendment does specifically limit the taxing and spending power conferred by Art. I, § 8. Whether the Constitution contains other specific limitations can be determined only in the context of future cases. However, whenever such specific limitations are found, we believe a taxpayer will have a clear stake as taxpayer in assuring that they are not breached by Congress. Consequently, we hold that a taxpayer will have standing consistent with Article III to invoke federal judicial power when he alleges that congressional action under the taxing and spending clause is in derogation of those constitutional provisions which operate to restrict the exercise of the taxing and spending power.

While we express no view at all on the merits of appellant's claims in this case, their complaint contains sufficient allegations under the criteria we have outlined to give them standing to invoke a federal court's jurisdiction for an adjudication on the merits.

TILTON v. RICHARDSON.

403 U. S. 672

Decided June 28, 1971 — four Justices dissenting.

Mr. Chief Justice BURGER announced the judgment of the Court . . .

This appeal presents important constitutional questions as to federal aid for church-related colleges and universities under Title I of the Higher Education Facilities Act of 1963 . . . which provides construction grants for buildings and facilities used exclusively for secular educational purposes. We must determine first whether the Act authorizes aid to such church-related institutions, and, if so, whether the Act violates either the Establishment or Free Exercise Clauses of the First Amendment.

The Higher Education Facilities Act . . . authorizes federal grants and loans to "institutions of higher education" for the construction of a wide variety of "academic facilities." But . . . expressly excludes

> "any facility used or to be used for sectarian instruction or as a place for religious worship, or . . . any facility which . . . is used or to be used primarily in connection with any part of the program of a school or department of divinity . . ."

The United States ratains a 20-year interest in any facility constructed with Title I funds. If, during this period, the recipient violates the statutory conditions, the United States is entitled to recover an amount equal to the proportion of its present value that the federal grant bore to the original cost of the facility.

We are satisfied that Congress intended the Act to include all colleges and universities regardless of any affiliation with or sponsorship by a religious body.

This interpretation is fully supported by the legislative history. Although there was extensive debate on the wisdom and constitutionality of aid to institutions affiliated with religious organizations, Congress clearly included them in the program.

Numerous cases considered by the Court have noted the internal tension in the First Amendment between the Establishment Clause and the Free Exercise Clause. *Walz v. Tax Comm'n*, 397 U. S. 664 (1970), is the most recent decision seeking to define the boundaries of the neutral area between these two provisions within which the legislature may legitimately act. There, as in other decisions, the Court treated the three main concerns against which the Establishment Clause sought to protect: "sponsorship, financial support, and active involvement of the soverign in religious activity."

Every analysis must begin with the candid acknowledgement that there is no single constitutional caliper that can be used to measure the precise degree to which these three factors are present or absent. Instead, our analysis in this area must begin with a consideration of the cumulative criteria developed over many years and applying to a wide range of governmental action challenged as violative of the Establishment Clause.

There are always risks in treating criteria discussed by the Court from time to time as "tests" in any limiting sense of that term. Constitutional adjudication does not lend itself to the absolutes of the physical sciences or mathematics. The standards should rather be viewed as guidelines with which to identify instances in which the objectives of the Religion Clauses have been impaired.

Against this background we consider four questions: First, does the Act reflect a secular legislative purpose? Second, is the primary effect of the Act to advance or inhibit religion? Third, does the administration of the Act foster an **excessive government entanglement with religion?** Fourth, does the implementation of the Act inhibit the free exercise of religion?

The stated legislative purpose appears in the preamble where Congress found and declared that

> "the security and welfare of the United States require that this and future

generations of American youth be assured ample opportunity for the fullest development of their intellectual capacities, and that this opportunity will be jeopardized unless the Nation's colleges and universities are encouraged and assisted in their efforts to accommodate rapidly growing numbers of youth who aspire to a higher education."

This expresses a legitimate secular objective entirely appropriate for governmental action.

The simplistic argument that every form of financial aid to church-sponsored activity violates the Religion Clauses was rejected long ago in *Bradfield v. Roberts*, 175 U.S. 291 (1899). . . . Construction grants surely aid these institutions in the sense that the construction of buildings will assist them to perform their various functions. But bus transportation, textbooks, and tax exemptions all gave aid in the sense that religious bodies would otherwise have been forced to find other sources from which to finance these services. Yet all of these forms of governmental assistance have been upheld. . . . The crucial question is not whether some benefit accrues to a religious institution as a consequence of the legislative program, but whether its principal or primary effect advances religion.

The Act itself was carefully drafted to ensure that the federally subsidized facilities would be devoted to the secular and not the religious function of the recipient institutions.

Finally, this record fully supports the findings of the District Court that none of the four church-related institutions in this case has violated the statutory restrictions.

Appellants instead rely on the argument that government may not subsidize any activities of an institution of higher learning that in some of its programs teaches religious doctrines. This argument rests on *Everson* . . . In *Allen*, however, it was recognized that the Court had fashioned criteria under which an analysis of a statute's purpose and effect was determinative as to whether religion was being advanced by government action.

Under this concept appellants' position depends on the validity of the proposition that religion so permeates the secular education provided by church-related colleges and universities that their religious and secular educational functions are in fact inseparable.

There is no evidence that religion seeps into the use of any of these facilities.

Although we reject appellants' broad constitutional arguments we do perceive an aspect in which the statute's enforcement provisions are inadequate to ensure that the impact of the federal aid will not advance religion. If a recipient institution violates any of the statutory restrictions on the use of a federally financed facility, § 754(b) (2) permits the Government to recover an amount equal to the proportion of the facility's present value that the federal grant bore to its original cost.

This remedy, however, is available to the Government only if the statutory conditions are violated "within twenty years after completion of construction."

Limiting the prohibition for religious use of the structure to 20 years obviously opens the facility to use for any purpose at the end of that period. It cannot be assumed that a substantial structure has no value after that period and hence the unrestricted use of a valuable property is in effect a contribution of some value to a religious body.

To this extent the Act therefore trespasses on the Religion Clauses. The restrictive obligations of a recipient institution . . . cannot, compatibly with the Religion Clauses, expire while the building has substantial value. This circumstance does not require us to invalidate the entire Act, however.

We have found nothing in the statute or its objectives intimating that Congress considered the 20-year provision essential to the statutory program as a whole.

We next turn to the question of whether excessive entanglements characterize the relationship between government and church under the Act.

There are generally significant differences between the religious aspects of church-related institutions of higher learning and parochial elementary and secondary schools. The "affirmative if not dominant policy" of the instruction in pre-college church schools is "to assure future adherents to a particular faith by having control of their total education at an early age."... There is substance to the contention that college students are less impressionable and less susceptible to religious indoctrination. . . . by their very nature, college and postgraduate courses tend to limit the opportunities for sectarian influence by virtue of their own internal disciplines. Many church-related colleges and universities are characterized by a high degree of academic freedom, and seek to evoke free and critical responses from their students.

The record here would not support a conclusion that any of these four institutions departed from this general pattern.

Since religious indoctrination is not a substantial purpose or activity of these church-related colleges and universities, there is less likelihood than in primary and secondary schools that religion will permeate the area of secular education. This reduces the risk that government aid will in fact serve to support religious activities. Correspondingly, the necessity for intensive government surveillance is diminished and the resulting entanglements between government and religion lessened.

The entanglement between church and state is also lessened here by the nonideological character of the aid that the Government provides. Our cases from *Everson* to *Allen* have permitted church-related schools to receive government aid in the form of secular, neutral, or nonideological services, facilities, or materials that are supplied to all students regardless of the affiliation of the school that they attend.

. . . the Government aid here is a one-time, single-purpose construction grant. There are no continuing financial relationships or dependencies, no annual audits, and no government analysis of an institution's expenditures on secular as distinguished from religious activities. Inspection as to use is a minimal contact.

Finally, we must consider whether the implementation of the Act inhibits the free exercise of religion in violation of the First Amendment. Appellants claim that the Free Exercise Clause is violated because they are compelled to pay taxes, the proceeds of which in part finance grants under the Act. . . . Their share of the cost of the grants under the Act is not fundamentally distinguishable from the impact of the tax exemption sustained in *Walz* or the provision of textbooks upheld in *Allen*.

We conclude that the Act does not violate the Religion Clauses of the First Amendment except that part . . . providing a 20-year limitation on the religious use restrictions contained in § 751 (a) (2).

Mr. Justice DOUGLAS, with whom Mr. Justice BLACK and Mr. Justice MARSHALL concur, dissenting in part.

The reversion of the facility to the parochial school at the end of 20 years is an outright grant, measurable by the present discounted worth of the facility. A gift of taxpayers' funds in that amount would plainly be unconstitutional.

But the invalidation of this one clause cannot cure the constitutional infirmities of the statute as a whole. The Federal Government is giving religious schools a block grant to build certain facilities.

The facilities financed by taxpayers' funds are not to be used for "sectarian" purposes. Religious teaching and secular teaching are so enmeshed in parochial schools that only the strictest supervision and surveillance would insure compliance with the condition. . . . A parochial school operates on one budget. Money not spent for one purpose becomes available for other purposes. Thus the fact that there are not religious observances in federally financed facilities is not controlling because required religious observances will take place in other buildings.

. . . surveillance creates an entanglement of government and religion which the First Amendment was designed to avoid. Yet after today's decision there will be a requirement of surveillance which will last for the useful life of the building and as we have previously noted, "[it] is hardly lack of due process for the Government to regulate that which it subsidizes.". . . How can the Government know what is taught in the federally financed building without a continuous auditing of classroom instruction? Yet both the Free Exercise Clause and academic freedom are violated when the Government agent must be present to determine whether the course content is satisfactory.

I dissent not because of any lack of respect for parochial schools but out of a feeling of despair that the respect which through history has been accorded the First Amendment is this day lost.

LEMON v. KURTZMAN.

EARLEY v. DiCENSO.

ROBINSON v. DiCENSO.

403 U. S. 602

Decided June 28, 1971 — one Justice dissenting in the Rhode Island decision.

Mr. Chief Justice BURGER delivered the opinion of the Court.

These two appeals raise questions as to Pennsylvania and Rhode Island statutes providing state aid to church-related elementary and secondary schools. Both statutes are challenged as violative of the Establishment and Free Exercise Clauses of the First Amendment and the Due Process Clause of the Fourteenth Amendment.

Pennsylvania has adopted a statutory program that provides financial support to nonpublic elementary and secondary schools by way of reimbursement for the cost of teachers' salaries, textbooks, and instructional mateials in specified secular subjects. Rhode Island has adopted a statute under which the State pays directly to teachers in nonpublic elementary schools a supplement of 15% of their annual salary. Under each statute state aid has been given to church-related educational institutions. We hold that both statutes are unconstitutional.

In *Everson v. Board of Education*, 330 U. S. 1 (1947), this Court upheld a state statute that reimbursed the parents of parochial school children for bus transportation expenses. There Mr. Justice Black, writing for the majority, suggested that the decision carried to "the verge" of forbidden territory under the Religion Clauses. . . . Candor compels acknowledgement, moreover, that we can only dimly perceive the lines of demarcation in this extraordinarily sensitive area of constitutional law.

The language of the Religion Clauses of the First Amendment is at best opaque, particularly when compared with other portions of the Amendment. Its authors did not simply prohibit the establishment of a state church or a state religion . . . Instead they commanded that there should be "no law *respecting* an establishment of religion.". . . A given law might not *establish* a state religion but nevertheless be one "respecting" that end in the sense of being a step that could lead to such establishment and hence offend the First Amendment.

In the absence of precisely stated constitutional prohibitions, we must draw lines with reference to the three main evils against which the Establishment Clause was intended to afford protection: "sponsorship, financial support, and active involvement of the soverign in religious activity."

Every analysis in this area must begin with consideration of the cumulative criteria developed by the Court over many years. Three such tests may be gleaned from our cases. First, the statute must have a secular legislative purpose; second, its principal or primary effect must be one that neither advances nor inhibits religion . . . finally, the statute must not foster "an excessive government entanglement with religion."

Inquiry into the legislative purposes of the Pennsylvania and Rhode Island statutes affords no basis for a conclusion that the legislative intent was to advance religion. On the contrary, the statutes themselves clearly state that they are intended to enhance the quality of the secular education in all schools covered by the compulsory attendance laws. There is no reason to believe the legislatures meant anything else.

The two legislatures, however, have also recognized that church-related elementary and secondary schools have a significant religious mission and that a substantial portion of their activities is religiously oriented. They have therefore sought to create statutory restrictions designed to guarantee the separation between secular and religious educational functions and to ensure that State financial aid supports only the former. . . . We need not decide whether these legislative precautions restrict the principal or primary effect of the programs to the point where they do not offend the Religion Clauses, for we conclude that the cumulative impact of the entire relationship arising under the statutes in each State involves excessive entanglement between government and religion.

In order to determine whether the government entanglement with religion is excessive, we must examine the character and purposes of the institutions that are benefited, the nature of the aid that the State provides, and the resulting relationship between the government and the religious authority.

Our decisions from *Everson* to *Allen* have permitted the States to provide church-related schools with secular, neutral, or nonideological services, facilities, or materials. Bus transportation, school lunches, public health services, and secular textbooks supplied in common to all students were not thought to offend the Establishment Clause.

In *Allen* the Court refused to make assumptions, on a meager record, about the religious content of the textbooks that the State would be asked to provide. We cannot, however, refuse here to recognize that teachers have a substantially different ideological character from books. In terms of potential for involving some aspect of faith or morals in secular subjects, a textbook's content is ascertainable, but a teacher's handling of a subject is not. We cannot ignore the danger that a teacher under religious control and discipline poses to the separation of the religious from the purely secular aspects of precollege education. The conflict of functions inheres in the situation.

In our view the record shows these dangers are present to a substantial degree.

The teacher is employed by a religious organization, subject to the direction and discipline of religious authorities, and works in a system dedicated to rearing children in a particular faith. These controls are not lessened by the fact that most of the lay teachers are of the Catholic faith. Inevitably some of a teacher's responsibilities hover on the border between secular and religious orientation.

We need not and do not assume that teachers in parochial schools will be guilty of bad faith or any conscious design to evade the limitations imposed by the statute and the First Amendment. We simply recognize that a dedicated religious person, teaching in a school affiliated with his or her faith and operated to inculcate its tenets, will inevitably experinece great difficulty in remaining religiously neutral.

A comprehensive, discriminating, and continuing state surveillance will inevitably be required to ensure that these restrictions are obeyed and the First Amendment otherwise respected. Unlike a book, a teacher cannot be inspected once so as to determine the extent and intent of his or her personal beliefs and subjective acceptance of the limitations imposed by the First Amendment.

There is another area of entanglement in the Rhode Island program that gives concern. The statute excludes teachers employed by nonpublic schools whose average per-pupil expenditures on secular education equal or exceed the comparable figures for public schools. In the event that the total expenditures of an otherwise eligible school exceed this norm, the program requires the government to examine the school's records in order to determine how much of the total expenditures is attributable to secular education and how much to religious activity. This kind of state inspection and evaluation of the religious content of a religious organization is fraught with the sort of entanglement that the Constitution forbids. It is a relationship pregnant with dangers of excessive government direction of church schools and hence of churches.

As we noted earlier, the very restrictions and surveillance necessary to ensure that teachers play a strictly nonideological role give rise to entanglements between church and state. The Pennsylvania statute, like that of Rhode Island, fosters this kind of relationship.

The Pennsylvania statute, moreover, has the further defect of providing state financial aid directly to the church-related schools. This factor distinguishes both *Everson* and *Allen*, for in both those cases the Court was careful to point out that state aid was provided to the student and his parents — not to the church-related school. . . . The history of government grants of a continuing cash subsidy indicates that such programs have almost always been accompanied by varying measures of control and surveillance. The government cash grants before us now provide no basis for predicting that comprehensive measures of surveillance and controls will not follow.

A broader base of entanglement of yet a different character is presented by the divisive political potential of these state programs. In a community where such a large number of pupils are served by church-related schools, it can be assumed that state assistance will entail considerable political activity. Partisans of parochial schools, understandably concerned with rising costs and sincerely dedicated to both the religious and secular educational missions of their schools, will inevitably champion this cause and promote political action to achieve their goals. Those who oppose state aid, whether for constitutional, religious, or fiscal reasons, will inevitably respond and employ all of the usual political campaign techniques to prevail. Candidates will be forced to declare and voters to choose. It would be unrealistic to ignore the fact that many people confronted with issues of this kind will find their votes aligned with their faith.

Ordinarily political debate and division, however vigorous or even partisan, are normal and healthy manifestations of our democratic system of government, but political division along religious lines was one of the principal evils against which the First Amendment was intended to protect. . . . We have an expanding array of vexing issues, local and national, domestic and international, to debate and divide on. It conflicts with our whole history and tradition to permit questions of the Religion Clauses to assume such importance in our legislatures and in our elections that they could divert attention from the myriad issues and problems that confront every level of government.

The potential for political divisiveness related to religious belief and practice is aggravated in these two statutory programs by the need for continuing annual appropriations and the likelihood of larger and larger demands as costs and populations grow.

We have no long history of state aid to church-related educational institutions comparable to 200 years of tax exemption for churches. Indeed, the state programs before us today represent something of an innovation. We have already noted that modern governmental programs have self-perpetuating and self-expanding propensities. These internal pressures are only enhanced when the schemes involve institutions whose legitimate needs are growing and whose interests have substantial political support. Nor can we fail to see that in constitutional adjudication some steps, which when taken were thought to approach "the verge," have become the platform for yet further steps. A certain momentum develops in constitutional theory and it can be a "downhill thrust" easily set in motion but difficult to retard or stop. Development by momentum is not invariably bad . . . but it is a force to be recognized and reckoned with.

. . . nothing we have said can be construed to disparage the role of church-related elementary and secondary schools in our national life. Their contribution has been and is enormous. Nor do we ignore their economic plight in a period of rising costs and expanding need. Taxpayers generally have been spared vast sums by the maintenance of these educational institutions by religious organizations, largely by the gifts of faithful adherents.

The merit and benefits of these schools, however, are not the issue before us in these cases. The sole question is whether state aid to these schools can be squared with the dictates of the Religion Clauses. Under our system the choice has been made that government is to be entirely excluded from the area of religious instruction and churches excluded from the affairs of government. The Constitution decrees that religion must be a private matter for the individual, the family, and the institutions of private choice, and that while some involvement and entanglement are inevitable, lines must be drawn.

Mr. Justice DOUGLAS, whom Mr. Justice BLACK joins, concurring.

The analysis of the constitutional objections to these two state systems of grants to parochial or sectarian schools must start with the admitted and obvious fact that the *raison d'etre* of parochial schools is the propagation of a religious faith. They also teach secular subjects; but they came into existence in this country because Protestant groups were perverting the public schools by using them to propagate their faith. The Catholics naturally rebelled. If schools were to be used to propagate a particular creed or religion, then Catholic ideals should also be served. Hence the advent of parochial schools.

The constitutional right of dissenters to substitute their parochial schools for public schools was sustained by the Court in *Pierce v. Society of Sisters*, 268 U. S. 510.

The story of conflict and dissension is long and well known. The result was a state of so-called equilibrium where religious instruction was eliminated from public schools and the use of public funds to support religious schools was deemed to be banned.

But the hydraulic pressures created by political forces and by economic stress were great and they began to change the situation.

And so we have gradually edged into a situation where vast amounts of public funds are supplied each year to sectarian schools.

While the evolution of the public school system in this country marked an escape from denominational control and was therefore admirable as seen through the eyes of those who think like Madison and Jefferson, it has disadvantages. The main one is that a state system may attempt to mold all students alike according to the views of the dominant group and to discourage the emergence of individual idiosyncrasies.

Sectarian education, however, does not remedy that condition. The advantages of sectarian education relate solely to religious or doctrinal matters.

We too have surveillance over sectarian schools but only to the extent of making sure that minimum educational standards are met, viz., competent teachers, accreditation of the school for diplomas, the number of hours of work and credits allowed, and so on.

But we have never faced, until recently, the problem of policing sectarian schools.

Public financial support of parochial schools puts those schools under disabilities with which they were not previously burdened.

Where the governmental activity is the financing of the private school, the various limitations or restraints imposed by the Constitution on state governments come into play.... Whatever might be the result in case of grants to students, it is clear that once one of the States finances a private school, it is duty-bound to make certain that the school stays within secular bounds and does not use the public funds to promote sectarian causes.

The intrusion of government into religious schools through grants, supervision, or surveillance may result in establishment of religion in the constitutional sense when what the State does enthrones a particular sect for overt or subtle propagation of its faith. Those activities of the State may also intrude on the Free Exercise Clause by depriving a teacher, under threats of reprisals, of the right to give sectarian construction or interpretation of, say, history and literature, or to use the teaching of such subjects to inculcate a religious creed or dogma.

Sectarian instruction, in which, of course, a State may not indulge, can take place in a course on Shakespeare or in one on mathematics. No matter what the curriculum offers, the question is, what is *taught?* We deal not with evil teachers but with zealous ones who may use any opportunity to indoctrinate a class.

It is well known that everything taught in most parochial schools is taught with the ultimate goal of religious education in mind.

One can imagine what a religious zealot, as contrasted to a civil libertairan, can do with the Reformation.or with the Inquisition.... I would think that policing these grants to detect sectarian instruction would be insufferable to religious partisans and would breed division and dissension between church and state.

In the present cases we deal with the totality of instruction destined to be sectarian, at least in part, if the religious character of the school is to be maintained. A school which operates to commingle religion with other instruction plainly cannot completely secularize its instruction. Parochial schools, in large measure, do not accept the assumption that secular subjects should be unrelated to religious teaching.

A history class, a literature class, or a science class in a parochial school is not a separate institute; it is part of the organic whole which the State subsidizes. The funds are used in these cases to pay or help pay the salaries of teachers in parochial schools; and the presence of teachers is critical to the essential purpose of the parochial school, *viz.*, to advance the religious endeavors of the particular church. It matters not that the teacher receiving taxpayers' money only teaches religion a fraction of the time. Nor does it matter that he or she teaches no religion. The school is an organism living on one budget. What the taxpayers give for salaries of those who teach only the humanities or science without any trace of proseletyzing enables the school to use all of its own funds for religious training.

Mr. Justice BRENNAN.

I agree that the judgments in Nos. 569 and 570 [*DiCenso*] must be affirmed. In my view the judgment in No. 89 [*Lemon*] must be reversed outright. I dissent in No. 153 [*Tilton*] . . .

The common feature of all three statutes before us is the provision of a direct subsidy from public funds for activities carried on by sectarian educational institutions.

The Nation's rapidly developing religious heterogeneity, the tide of Jacksonian democracy, and growing urbanization soon led to widespread demands throughout the States for secular public education. At the same time strong opposition developed to use of the States' taxing powers to support private sectarian schools. Although the controversy over religious exercises in the public schools continued into this century . . . the opponents of subsidy to sectarian schools had largely won their fight by 1900.

Policing the content of courses, the specific textbooks used, and indeed the words of teachers is far different from the legitimate policing carried on under state compulsory attendance laws or laws regulating minimum levels of educational achievement. Government's legitimate interest in ensuring certain minimum skill levels and the acquisition of certain knowledge does not carry with it power to prescribe what shall *not* be taught, or what methods or instruction shall be used, or what opinions the teacher may offer in the course of teaching.

The State's interest in secular education may be defined broadly as an interest in ensuring that all children within its boundaries acquire a minimum level of competency in certain skills, such as reading, writing, and arithemtic, as well as a minimum amount of information and knowledge in certain subjects such as history, geography, science, literature, and law. Without such skills and knowledge, an individual will be at a severe disadvantage both in participating in democratic self-government and in earning a living in a modern industrial economy. But the State has no proper interest in prescribing the precise forum in which such skills and knowledge are learned since acquisition of this secular education is neither incompatible with religious learning, nor is it inconsistent with or inimical to religious precepts.

When the same secular educational process occurs in both public and sectarian schools, *Allen* held that the State could provide secular textbooks for use in that process to students in both public and sectarian schools. Of course, the State could not provide textbooks giving religious instruction. But since the textbooks involved in *Allen* would, at least in theory, be limited to secular education, no aid to sectarian instruction was involved.

More important, since the textbooks in *Allen* had been previously provided by the parents, and not the schools . . . no aid to the institution was involved. Rather, as in the case of the bus transportation in *Everson*, the general program of providing all children in the State with free secular textbooks assisted all parents in schooling their children.

The present cases, however, involve direct subsidies of tax monies to the schools themselves and we cannot blink the fact that the secular education those schools provide goes hand in hand with the religious mission that is the only reason for the schools' existence. Within the institution, the two are inextricably intertwined.

The plurality's treatment of the issues in *Tilton* . . . diverges so substantially from my own that I add these further comments. I believe that the Establishment Clause forbids the Federal Government to provide funds to sectarian universities in which the propagation and advancement of a particular religion are a function or purpose of the institution.

I reach this conclusion for the reasons I have stated: the necessarily deep involvement of government in the religious activities of such an institution through the policing of restrictions, and the fact that subsidies of tax monies directly to a sectarian institution necessarily aid the proselytizing function of the institution.

. . . I emphasize that a sectarian university is the equivalent in the realm of higher education of the Catholic elementary schools in Rhode Island; it is an educational institution in which the propagation and advancement of a particular religion are a primary function of the institution. I do not believe that construction grants to such a sectarian institution are permissible. The reason is not that religion "permeates" the secular education that is provided. Rather, it is that the secular education is provided within the environment of religion; the institution is dedicated to two goals, secular education *and* religious instruction. When aid flows directly to the institution, both functions benefit.

Since I believe the statute's extension of eligibility to sectarian institutions is severable from the broad general program authorized, I would hold the Higher Education Facilities Act unconstitutional only insofar as it authorized grants of federal tax monies to sectarian institutions — institutions that have a purpose or function to propagate or advance a particular religion.

Mr. Justice WHITE, concurring in the judgments in 89 [*Lemon*] and 153 [*Tilton*] and dissenting in Nos. 569 and 570 [*DiCenso*].

It is our good fortune that the States of this country long ago recognized that instruction of the young and old ranks high on the scale of proper governmental functions and not only undertook secular education as a public responsibility but also required compulsory attendance at school by their young. Having recognized the value of educated citizens and assumed the task of educating them, the States now before us assert a right to provide for the secular education of children whether they attend public schools or choose to enter private institutions, even when those institutions are church-related. The Federal Government also asserts that it is entitled, where requested, to contribute to the cost of secular education by furnishing buildings and facilities to all institutions of higher learning, public and private alike. Both the United States and the States urge that if parents choose to have their children receive instruction in the required secular subjects in a school where religion is also taught and a religious atmosphere may prevail, part or all of the cost of such secular instruction may be paid for by governmental grants to the religious institution conducting the school and seeking the grant. Those who challenge this position would bar official contributions to secular education where the family prefers the parochial to both the public and nonsectarian private school.

Our prior cases have recognized the dual role of parochial schools in American society: they perform both religious and secular functions. . . . Our cases also recognize that legislation having a secular purpose and extending governmental assistance to sectarian schools in the performance of their secular functions does not constitute "law[s] respecting an establishment of religion" forbidden by the First Amendment merely because a secular program may incidentally benefit a church in fulfilling its religious mission. That religion may indirectly benefit from governmental aid to the secular activities of churches does not convert that aid into an impermissible establishment of religion.

It is enough for me that the States and the Federal Government are financing a separable secular function of overriding importance in order to sustain the legislation here challenged. That religion and private interests other than education may substantially benefit does not convert these laws into impermissible establishments of religion.

I would sustain both the federal and the Rhode Island programs at issue in these cases, and I therefore concur in the judgment in No. 153 and dissent from the judgments in Nos. 569 and 570. Although I would also reject the facial challenge to the Pennsylvania statute, I concur in the judgment in No. 89 for the reasons given below.

The Court strikes down the Rhode Island statute on its face. No fault is found with the secular purpose of the program . . . Nor does the Court find that the primary effect of the program is to aid religion rather than to implement secular goals. The Court nevertheless finds that impermissible "entanglement" will result from administration of the program.

. . . the potential for impermissible fostering of religion in secular classrooms — an untested assumption of the Court — paradoxically renders unacceptable the State's efforts at insuring that secular teachers under religious discipline successfully avoid conflicts between the religious mission of the school and the secular purpose of the State's education program.

The difficulty with this is twofold. In the first place, it is contrary to the evidence and the District Court's findings in *DiCenso*. The Court points to nothing in this record indicating that any participating teacher had inserted religion into his secular teaching or had had any difficulty in avoiding doing so.

Secondly, the Court accepts the model for the Catholic elementary and secondary schools that was rejected for the Catholic universities or colleges in the *Tilton* case.

The Court thus creates an insoluble paradox for the State and the parochial schools. The State cannot finance secular instruction if it permits religion to be taught in the same classroom; but if it exacts a promise that religion not be so taught — a promise the school and its teachers are quite willing and on this record able to give — and enforces it, it is then entangled in the "no entanglement" aspect of the Court's Establishment Clause jurisprudence.

Why the federal program in the *Tilton* case is not embroiled in the same difficulties is never adequately explained. Surely the notion that college students are more mature and resistant to indoctrination is a make-weight . . .

[With respect to Pennsylvania] There is no specific allegation in the complaint that sectarian teaching does or would invade secular classes supported by state funds. That the schools are operated to promote a particular religion is quite consistent with the view that secular teaching devoid of religious instruction can successfully be maintained, for good secular instruction is . . . essential to the success of the religious mission of the parochial school. I would no more here than in the Rhode Island case substitute presumption for proof that religion is or would be taught in state-financed secular courses or assume that enforcement measures would be so extensive as to border on a free exercise violation.

I do agree, however, that the complaint should not have been dismissed for failure to state a cause of action. Although it did not specifically allege that the schools involved mixed religious teaching with secular subjects, the complaint did allege that the schools were operated to fulfill religious purposes and one of the legal theories stated in the complaint was that the Pennsylvania Act "finances and participates in the blending of sectarian and secular instruction."... Hence, I would reverse the judgment of the District Court and remand the case for trial, thereby holding the Pennsylvania legislation valid on its face but leaving open the question of its validity as applied to the particular facts of this case.

I find it . . . difficult . . . to understand how the Court can accept the considered judgment of Congress that its program is constitutional and yet reject the equally considered decisions of the Rhode Island and Pennsylvania legislatures that their programs represent a constitutionally acceptable accommodation between church and state.

LEMON v. KURTZMAN.

411 U. S. 192

Decided April 2, 1973 — three Justices dissenting.

Mr. Chief Justice BURGER announced the judgment of the Court . . .

On June 28, 1971, we held that the Pennsylvania statutory program to reimburse nonpublic sectarian schools for certain secular educational services violated the Establishment Clause of the First Amendment. The case was remanded to the three-judge District Court for further proceedings consistent with our opinion. . . . The District Court's order premitted the State to reimburse nonpublic sectarian schools for services provided before our decision in *Lemon I*. Appellants made no claim that appellees refund all sums paid under the Pennsylvania statute struck down in *Lemon I*.

Appellants, the successful plaintiffs of *Lemon I*, now challenge the limited scope of the District Court's injunction. Specifically, they assert that the District Court erred in refusing to enjoin payment of some $24 million set aside by Pennsylvania to compensate nonpublic sectarian schools for educational services rendered by them during the 1970-1971 school year.

The sensitive values of the Religion Clauses do not readily lend themselves to quantification but, despite the inescapable imprecision, we think it clear that the proposed distribution of state funds to Pennsylvania's nonpublic sectarian schools will not substantially undermine the constitutional interests at stake in *Lemon I*.

There is no present risk of significant intrusive administrative entanglement, since only a final post-audit remains and detailed state surveillance of the schools is a thing of the past. At the same time, that very process of oversight — now an accomplished fact — assures that state funds will not be applied for any sectarian purposes.

Offsetting the remote possibility of constitutional harm from allowing the State to keep its bargain are the expenses incurred by the schools in reliance on the state statute inviting the contracts made and authorizing reimbursement for past services performed by the schools.

That there would be constitutional attack on Act 109 was plain from the outset. But this is not a case where it could be said that appellees acted in bad faith or that they relied on a plainly unlawful statute.

In the end, then, appellants' position comes down to this: that any reliance whatever by the schools was unjustified because Act 109 was an "untested" state statute whose validity had never been authoritatively determined. The short answer to this argument is that governments must act if they are to fulfill their high responsibilities.

Appellants would have state officials stay their hands until newly enacted state programs are "ratified" by the federal courts, or risk draconian, retrospective decrees should the legislation fail. In our view, appellants' position could seriously undermine the initiative of state legislators and executive officials alike. Until judges say otherwise, state officers — the officers of Pennsylvania — have the power to carry forward the directives of the state legislature. Those officials may, in some circumstances, elect to defer acting until an authoritative judicial pronouncement has been secured; but particularly when there are no fixed and clear constitutional precedents, the choice is essentially one of political discretion and one this Court has never conceived as an incident of judicial review.

*LEVITT v. COMMITTEE FOR PUBLIC
EDUCATION AND RELIGIOUS LIBERTY.*

*ANDERSON v. COMMITTEE FOR PUBLIC
EDUCATION AND RELIGIOUS LIBERTY.*

*CATHEDRAL ACADEMY v. COMMITTEE FOR
PUBLIC EDUCATION AND RELIGIOUS
LIBERTY.*

413 U. S. 472

Decided June 25, 1973 — one Justice dissenting.

Mr. Chief Justice BURGER delivered the opinion of the Court.

We are asked to decide whether Chapter 138 of New York State's Laws of 1970 under which the State reimburses private schools throughout the State for certain costs of testing and recordkeeping, violates the Establishment Clause of the First Amendment.

. . . the State has in essence sought to reimburse private schools for performing various "services" which the State "mandates." Of these mandated services, by far the most expensive for nonpublic schools is the "administration, grading and the compiling and reporting of the results of tests and examinations." Such "tests and examinations" appear to be of two kinds: (a) state-prepared examinations, such as the "Regents examinations" and the "Pupil Evaluation Program Tests," and (b) traditional teacher-prepared tests, which are drafted by the nonpublic school teachers for the purpose of measuring the pupils' progress in subjects required to be taught under state law. The overwhelming majority of testing in nonpublic, as well as public, schools, is of the latter variety.

Church-sponsored as well as secular nonpublic schools are eligible to receive payments under the Act.

Qualifying schools receive an annual payment of $27 for each pupil in average daily attendance in grades one through six and $45 for each pupil in average daily attendance in grades seven through 12.

Section 8 of the Act states: "Nothing contained in this act shall be construed to authorize the making of any payment under this act for religious worship or instruction." However, the Act contains no provision authorizing state audits of school financial records to determine whether a school's actual costs in complying with the mandated services are less than the annual lump sum payment. Nor does the Act require a school to return to the State moneys received in excess of its actual expenses.

Appellees are New York taxpayers and an unincorporated association. They filed this suit in the United States District Court claiming that Chapter 138 abridges the Establishment Clause of the First Amendment.

We cannot ignore the substantial risk that these examinations, prepared by teachers under the authority of religious institutions, will be drafted with an eye, unconsciously or otherwise, to inculcate students in the religious precepts of the sponsoring church. We do not "assume that teachers in parochial schools will be guilty of bad faith or any conscious design to evade the limitations imposed by the statute and the First Amendment.". . . But the potential for conflict "inheres in the situation," and because of that the State is constitutionally compelled to assure that the state-supported activity is not being used for religious indoctrination. . . . Since the State has failed to do so here, we are left with no choice under *Nyquist* but to hold that Chapter 138 constitutes an impermissible aid to reigion; this is so because the aid that will be devoted to secular functions is not identifiable and separable from aid to sectarian activities.

To the extent that appellants argue that the State should be permitted to pay for any activity "mandated" by state law or regulation, we must reject the contention.

We hold that the lump-sum payments under Chapter 138 violate the Establishment Clause. Since Chapter 138 provides only for a single per-pupil allotment for a variety of specified services, some secular and some potentially religious, neither this Court nor the District Court can properly reduce that allotment to an amount corresponding to the actual costs incurred in performing reimbursable secular services. That is a legislative, not a judicial, function.

HUNT v. McNAIR.

413 U. S. 734

Decided June 25, 1973 — three Justices dissenting.

Mr. Justice POWELL delivered the opinion of the Court.

Appellant, a South Carolina taxpayer, brought this action to challenge the South Carolina Educational Facilities Authority Act . . . as violative of the Establishment Clause of the First Amendment insofar as it authorizes a proposed financing transaction involving the issuance of revenue bonds for the benefit of the Baptist College at Charleston.

The Act established an Educational Facilities Authority . . . the purpose of which is "to assist institutions for higher education in the construction, financing and refinancing of projects . . ." primarily through the issuance of revenue bonds. Under the terms of the Act, a project may encompass buildings, facilities, site preparation, and related items, but may not include "any facility used or to be used for sectarian instruction or as a place of religious worship nor any facility which is used or to be used primarily in connection with any part of the program of a school or department of divinity for any religious denomination."

While revenue bonds to be used in connection with a project are issued by the Authority, the Act is quite explicit that the bonds shall not be obligations of the State, directly or indirectly . . . Moreover, since all of the expenses of the Authority must be paid from the revenues of the various projects in which it participates . . . none of the general revenues of South Carolina is used to support a project.

The purpose of the statute is manifestly a secular one. The benefits of the Act are available to all institutions of higher education in South Carolina, whether or not having a religious affiliation.

To idenfity "primary effect," we narrow our focus from the statute as a whole to the only transaction presently before us. Whatever may be its initial appeal, the proposition that the Establishment Clause prohibits any program which in some manner aids an institution with a religious affiliation has consistently been rejected. . . . Stated another way, the Court has not accepted the recurrent argument that all aid is forbidden because aid to one aspect of an institution frees it to spend its other resources on religious ends.

Aid normally may be thought to have a primary effect of advancing religion when it flows to an institution in which religion is so pervasive that a substantial portion of its functions are subsumed in the religious mission or when it funds a specifically religious activity in an otherwise substantially secular setting.

Appellant has introduced no evidence in the present case placing the College in such a category. . . . On the record in this case there is no basis to conclude that the College's operations are oriented significantly towards sectarian rather than secular education.

Nor can we conclude that the proposed transaction will place the Authority in the position of providing aid to the religious as opposed to the secular activities of the College. The scope of the Authority's power to assist institutions of higher education extends only to "projects," and the Act specifically states that a project "shall not include" any buildings or facilities used for religious purposes. In the absence of evidence to the contrary, we must assume that all of the proposed financing and refinancing relates to buildings and facilities within a properly delimited project.

The final question posed by this case is whether under the arrangement there would be an unconstitutional degree of entanglement between the State and the College. Appellant argues that the Authority would become involved in the operation of the College both by inspecting the project to insure that it is not being used for religious purposes and by participating in the management decisions of the College.

The Court's opinion in *Lemon* and the plurality opinion in *Tilton* are grounded on the proposition that the degree of entanglement arising from inspection of facilities as to use varies in large measure with the extent to which religion permeates the institution.

A majority of the Court in *Tilton*, then, concluded that on the facts of that case inspection as to use did not threaten excessive entanglement. As we have indicated above, there is no evidence here to demonstrate that the College is any more an instrument of religious indoctrination than were the colleges and universities involved in *Tilton*.

A closer issue under our precedents is presented by the contention that the Authority could become deeply involved in the day-to-day financial and policy decisions of the College.

. . . under the proposed Lease Agreement, neither the Authority nor a trustee bank would be justified in taking action unless the College fails to make the prescribed rental payments or otherwise defaults in its obligatons. Only if the College refused to meet rental payments or was unable to do so would the Authority or the trustee be obligated to take further action. In that event, the Authority or trustee might either foreclose on the mortgage or take a hand in the setting of rules, charges, and fees. It may be argued that only the former would be consistent with the Establishment Clause, but we do not now have that situation before us.

The specific provisions of the Act under which the bonds will be issued, the Rules and Regulations of the Authority, and the College's proposal — all as interpreted by the South Carolina Supreme Court — confine the scope of the assistance to the secular aspects of this liberal arts college and do not foreshadow excessive entanglement between the State and religion. Accordingly, we affirm the holding of the court below that the Act is constitutional as interpreted and applied in this case.

Mr. Justice BRENNAN, with whom Mr. Justice DOUGLAS and Mr. Justice MARSHALL join, dissenting.

The arrangement does not . . . amount merely to a mortgage on the campus property. The Authority is also empowered, *inter alia*, to determine the location and character of any project financed under the act; to construct, maintain, manage, operate, lease as lessor or lessee, and regulate the same; to enter into contracts for the management and operation of such project; to establish rules and regulations for the use of the project or any portion thereof; and to fix and revise from time to time rates, rents, fees, and charges for the use of a project and for the services furnished or to be furnished by a project or any portion thereof. In other words, the College turns over to the State Authority control of substantial parts of the fiscal operation of the school — its very life's blood.

. . . it is crystal clear, I think, that this scheme involves the State in a degree of policing of the affairs of the College far exceeding that called for by the statutes struck down in *Lemon I* . . . Indeed, under this scheme the policing by the State can become so extensive that the State may well end up in complete control of the operation of the College, at least for the life of the bonds. The College's freedom to engage in religious activities and to offer religious instruction is necessarily circumscribed by this pervasive state involvement forced upon the College if it is not to lose its beneifts under the Act. For it seems inescapable that the content of courses taught in facilities financed under the agreement must be closely monitored by the State Authority in discharge of its duty to ensure that the facilities are not being used for sectarian instruction. The Authority must also involve itself deeply in the fiscal affairs of the College, even to the point of fixing tuition rates, as part of its duty to assure sufficient revenues to meet bond and interest obligations. And should the College find itself unable to meet these obligations, its continued existence as a viable sectarian institution is almost completely in the hands of the State Authority.

In support of its contrary argument, the Court adopts much of the reasoning of the plurality opinion in *Tilton v. Richardson* . . . I disagreed with that reasoning in *Tilton* because, as in this case, that reasoning utterly failed to explain how programs of surveillance and inspection of the kind common to both cases differ from the Pennsylanvia and Rhode Island programs invalidated in *Lemon I.*

In short, the Couth Carolina statutory scheme as applied to this sectarian institution presents the very sort of "intimate continuing relationship or dependency between government and religiously affiliated institutions" that in the pluarlity's view was lacking in *Tilton* . . .

Nor is the South Carolina arrangement between the State and this College any less offensive to the Constitution because it involves, as the Court asserts, no direct financial support to the College by the State. The Establishment Clause forbids far more than payment of public funds directly to support sectarian institutions. It forbids any official involvement with religion, whatever its form, which tends to foster or discourage religious worship or belief.

The State forthrightly aids the College by permitting the College to avail itself of the State's unique ability to borrow money at low interest rates, and the College, in turn, surrenders to the State a comprehensive and continuing surveillance of the educational, religious, and fiscal affairs of the College. The conclusion is compelled that this involves the State in the "essentially religious activities of religious institutions" and "employ[s] the organs of government for essentially religious purposes." I therefore dissent and would reverse the judgment of the Supreme Court of South Carolina.

COMMITTEE FOR PUBLIC EDUCATION AND RELIGIOUS LIBERTY v. NYQUIST.

ANDERSON v. COMMITTEE FOR PUBLIC EDUCATION AND RELIGIOUS LIBERTY.

NYQUIST v. COMMITTEE FOR PUBLIC EDUCATION AND RELIGIOUS LIBERTY.

CHERRY v. COMMITTEE FOR PUBLIC EDUCATION AND RELIGIOUS LIBERTY.

413 U. S. 756

Decided June 25, 1973 — three Justices dissenting.

Mr. Justice POWELL delivered the opinion of the Court.

These cases raise a challenge under the Establishment Clause of the First Amendment to the constitutionality of a recently enacted New York law which provides financial assistance, in several ways, to nonpublic elementary and secondary schools in that State. The cases involve an intertwining of societal and constitutional issues of the greatest importance.

In May 1972, the Governor of New York signed into law several amendments to the State's Education and Tax Laws. The first five sections of these amendments established three distinct financial aid programs for nonpublic elementary and secondary schools.

The first section of the challenged enactment, entitled "Health and Safety Grants for Nonpublic School Children," provides for direct money grants from the State to "qualifying" nonpublic schools to be used for the "maintenance and repair of . . . school facilities and equipment to ensure the health, welfare and safety of enrolled pupils." A "qualifying" school is any nonpublic, nonprofit elementary or secondary school which "has been designated during the [immediately preceding] year as serving a high concentration of pupils from low-income families for purposes of Title IV of the Federal Higher Education Act of nineteen hundred sixty-five . . .

This section is prefaced by a series of legislative findings which shed light on the State's purpose in enacting the law. These findings conclude that the State "has a primary responsibility to ensure the health, welfare and safety of children attending . . . nonpublic schools"; that the "fiscal crisis in nonpublic education . . . has caused a diminution of proper maintenance and repair programs, threatening the health, welfare and safety of nonpublic school children" in low-income urban areas; and that "a healthy and safe school environment" contributes "to the stability of urban neighborhoods."

The remainder of the challenged legislation — §§ 2 through 5 — is a single package captioned the "Elementary and Secondary Education Opportunity Program." It is composed, essentially, of two parts, a tuition grant program and a tax benefit program. Section 2 establishes a limited plan providing tuition reimbursements to parents of children attending elementary or secondary nonpublic schools. To qualify under this section a parent must have an annual taxable income of less than $5,000.

This section, like § 1, is prefaced by a series of legislative findings designed to explain the impetus for the State's action. Expressing a dedication to the "vitality of our pluralistic society," the findings state that a "healthy competitive and diverse alternative to public education is not only desirable but indeed vital to a state and nation that have continually reaffirmed the value of individual differences." The findings further emphasize that the right to select among alternative educational systems "is diminished or even denied to children of lower-income families, whose parents, of all groups, have the least options in determining where their children are to be educated." Turning to the public schools, the findings state that any "precipitous decline in the number of nonpublic school pupils would cause a massive increase in public school enrollment and costs," an increase that would "aggravate an already serious fiscal crises in public education" and would "seriously jeopardize quality education for all children."

The remainder of the "Elementary and Secondary Education Opportunity Program," contained in §§ 3, 4, and 5 of the challenged law, is designed to provide a form of tax relief to those who fail to quality for tuition reimbursement. Under these sections parents may subtract from their adjusted gross income for state income tax purposes a designated amount for each dependent for whom they have paid at least $50 in nonpublic school tuition.

. . . § 3 does contain an additional series of legislative findings. Those findings may be summarized as follows: (i) contributions to religious, charitable and educational institutions are already deductible from gross income; (ii) nonpublic educational institutions are accorded tax exempt status; (iii) such institutions provide education for children attending them and also serve to relieve the public school systems of the burden of providing for their education; and, therefore, (iv) the "legislature . . . finds and determines that similar modifications . . . should also be provided to parents for tuition paid to nonpublic elementary and secondary schools on behalf of their dependents."

Plaintiffs argued below that because of the substantially religious character of the intended beneficiaries, each of the State's three enactments offended the Establishment Clause. . . . the constitutionality of each of New York's recently promulgated aid provisions is squarely before us. We affirm the District Court insofar as it struck down §§ 1 and 2 and reverse its determination regarding §§ 3, 4, and 5.

. . . it is now firmly established that a law may be one "respecting an establishment of religion" even though its consequence is not to promote a "state religion,". . . and even though it does not aid one religion more than another but merely benefits all religions alike. . . . It is equally well established, however, that not every law that confers an "indirect," "remote," or "incidental" benefit upon religious institutions is, for that reason alone, constitutionally invalid.

Most of the cases coming to this Court raising Establishment Clause questions have involved the relationship between religion and education. Among these religion-education precedents, two general categories of cases may be identified: those dealing with religious activities within the public schools, and those involving public aid in varying forms to sectarian educational institutions. While the New York legislation places this case in the latter category, its resolution requires consideration, not only of the several aid-to-sectarian-education cases, but also of our other education precedents and of several important non-education cases. . . . Taken together, these decisions dictate that to pass muster under the Establishment Clause the law in question first must reflect a clearly secular legislative purpose . . . second, must have a primary effect that neither advances nor inhibits religion . . . and, third, must avoid excessive government entanglement with religion . . .

In applying these criteria to the three distinct forms of aid involved in this case, we need touch only briefly on the requirement of a "secular legislative purpose."

As the recitation of legislative purposes appended to New York's law indicates, each measure is adequately supported by legitimate, nonsectarian state interests.

But the propriety of a legislature's purposes may not immunize from further scrutiny a law which either has a primary effect that advances religion, or which fosters excessive entanglements between Church and State.

The "maintenance and repair" provisions of § 1 authorize direct payments to nonpublic schools, virtually all of which are Roman Catholic schools in low-income areas. . . . No attempt is made to restrict payments to those expenditures related to the upkeep of facilities used exclusively for secular purposes, nor do we think it possible within the context of these religion-oriented institutions to impose such restrictions. Nothing in the statute, for instance, bars a qualifying school from paying out of state funds the salaries of employees who maintain the school chapel, or the cost of renovating classrooms in which religion is taught, or the cost of heating and lighting those same facilities. Absent appropriate restrictions on expenditures for these and similar purposes, it simply cannot be denied that this section has a primary effect that advances religion in that it subsidizes directly the religious activities of sectarian elementary and secondary schools.

In *Everson*, the Court, in a five-to-four decision, approved a program of reimbursements to parents of public as well as parochial schoolchildren for bus fares paid in connection with transportation to and from school, a program which the Court characterized as approaching the "verge" of impermissible state aid. . . . In *Allen*, decided some 20 years later, the Court upheld a New York law authorizing the provision of *secular* textbooks for all children in grades seven through 12 attending public and nonpublic schools. Finally, in *Tilton*, the Court upheld federal grants of funds for the construction of facilities to be used for clearly *secular* purposes by public and nonpublic institutions of higher learning.

These cases simply recognize that sectarian schools perform secular, educational functions as well as religious functions, and that some forms of aid may be channeled to the secular without providing direct aid to the sectarian. But the channel is a narrow one, as the above cases illustrate. . . . an indirect and incidental effect beneficial to religious institutions has never been thought a sufficient defect to warrant the invalidation of a state law.

Tilton draws the line most clearly. . . . If tax-raised funds may not be granted to institutions of higher learning where the possibility exists that those funds will be used to construct a facility utilized for sectarian activities 20 years hence, *a fortiori* they may not be distributed to elementary and secondary sectarian schools for the maintenance and repair of facilities without any limitations on their use. If the State may not erect buildings in which religious activities are to take place, it may not maintain such buildings or renovate them when they fall into disrepair.

It might be argued, however, that while the New York "maintenance and repair" grants lack specifically articulated secular restrictions, the statute does provide a sort of statistical guarantee of separation by limiting grants to 50% of the amount expended for comparable services in the public schools. . . . Quite apart from the language of the statute, our cases make clear that a mere statistical judgment will not suffice as a guarantee that state funds will not be used to finance religious education.

What we have said demonstrates that New York's maintenance and repair provisions violate the Establishment Clause because their effect, inevitably, is to subsidize and advance the religious mission of sectarian schools. We have no occasion, therefore, to consider the further question whether those provisions as presently written would also fail to survive scrutiny under the administrative entanglement aspect of the three-part test because assuring the secular use of all funds requires too intrusive and continuing a relationship between Church and State . . .

New York's tuition reimbursement program also fails the "effect" test, for much the same reasons that govern its maintenance and repair grants.

There can be no question that these grants could not, consistently with the Establishment Clause, be given directly to sectarian schools, since they would suffer from the same deficiency that renders invalid the grants for maintenance and repair. In the absence of an effective means of guaranteeing that the state aid derived from public funds will be used exclusively for secular, neutral, and nonideological purposes, it is clear from our cases that direct aid in whatever form is invalid. . . . The controlling question here, then, is whether the fact that the grants are delivered to parents rather than schools is of such significance as to compel a contrary result.

. . . it is precisely the function of New York's law to provide assistance to private schools, the great majority of which are sectarian. By reimbursing parents for a portion of their tuition bill, the State seeks to relieve their financial burdens sufficiently to assure that they continue to have the option to send their children to religion-oriented schools. And while the other purposes of that aid . . . are certainly unexceptionable, the effect of the aid is unmistakably to provide desired financial support for nonpublic, sectarian institutions.

. . . if the grants are offered as an incentive to parents to send their children to sectarian schools by making unrestricted cash payments to them, the Establishment Clause is violated whether or not the actual dollars given eventually find their way into the sectarian institutions.

. . . our cases require the State to maintain an attitude of "neutrality," neither "advancing" nor "inhibiting" religion. In its attempt to enhance the opportunities of the poor to choose between public and nonpublic education, the State has taken a step which can only be regarded as one "advancing" religion.

Sections 3, 4, and 5 establish a system for providing income tax benefits to parents of children attending New York's nonpublic schools.

In practical terms there would appear to be little difference, for purposes of determining whether such aid has the effect of advancing religion, between the tax benefit allowed here and the tuition grant allowed under § 2. The qualifying parent under either program receives the same form of encouragement and reward for sending his children to nonpublic schools. The only difference is that one parent receives an actual cash payment while the other is allowed to reduce by an arbitrary amount the sum he would otherwise be obliged to pay over to the State.

Appellees defend the tax portion of New York's legislative package on two grounds. First, they contend that it is of controlling significance that the grants or credits are directed to the parents rather than to the schools. This is the same argument made in support of the tuition reimbursements . . . Second, appellees place their strongest reliance on *Walz v. Tax Comm'n* . . . in which New York's property tax exemption for religious organizations was upheld. We think that *Walz* provides no support for appellees' position.

The Court in *Walz* surveyed the history of tax exemptions . . . In sum, the Court concluded that "[f]ew concepts are more deeply embedded in the fabric of our national life, beginning with pre-Revolutionary colonial times, than for the government to exercise at the very least this kind of benevolent neutrality toward churches and religious exercise generally.". . . We know of no historical precedent for New York's recently promulgated tax relief program.

But historical acceptance without more would not alone have sufficed . . . It was the reason underlying that long history of tolerance of tax exemptions for religion that proved controlling. A proper respect for both the Free Exercise and the Establishment Clauses compels the State to pursue a course of "neutrality" toward religion. Yet governments have not always pursued such a course, and oppression has taken many forms, one of which has been taxation of religion. Thus, if taxation was regarded as a form of "hostility" toward religion, "exemption constitute[d] a reasonable and balanced attempt to guard against those dangers.". . . Special tax benefits, however, cannot be squared with the principle of neutrality established by the decisions of this Court. To the contrary, insofar as such benefits render assistance to parents who send their children to sectarian schools, their purpose and inevitable effect are to aid and advance those religious institutions.

To be sure, the exemption of church property from taxation conferred a benefit, albeit an indirect and incidental one. Yet that "aid" was a product not of any purpose to support or to subsidize, but of a fiscal relationship designed to minimize involvement and entanglement between Church and State.

In conclusion, we find the *Walz* analogy unpersuasive, and in light of the practical similarity between New York's tax and tuition reimbursement programs, we hold that neither form of aid is sufficiently restricted to assure that it will not have the impermissible effect of advancing the sectarian activities of religious schools.

Because we have found that the challenged sections have the impermissible effect of advancing religion, we need not consider whether such aid would result in entanglement of the State with religion in the sense of "[a] comprehensive, discriminating, and continuing state surveillance.". . . But the importance of the competing societal interests implicated here prompts us to make the further observation that, apart from any specific entanglement of the State in particular religious programs, assistance of the sort here involved carries grave potential for entanglement in the broader sense of continuing political strife over aid to religion.

Few would question most of the legislative findings supporting this statute. . . . There is no doubt that the private schools are confronted with increasingly grave fiscal problems, that resolving these problems by increasing tuition charges forces parents to turn to the public schools, and that this in turn — as the present legislation recognizes — exacerbates the problems of public education at the same time that it weakens support for the parochial schools.

These, in briefest summary, are the underlying reasons for the New York legislation and for similar legislation in other States. They are substantial reasons. Yet they must be weighed against the relevant provisions and purposes of the First Amendment . . .

One factor of recurring significance in this weighting process is the potentially divisive political effect of an aid program.

The language of the Court applies with peculiar force to the New York statute now before us. Section 1 . . . and § 2 . . . will require continuing annual appropriations. Sections 3, 4, and 5 . . . will not necessarily require annual re-examination, but the pressure for frequent enlargement of the relief is predictable. All three of these programs start out at modest levels . . . But we know from long experience with both Federal and State Governments that aid programs of any kind tend to become entrenched, to escalate in cost, and to generate their own aggressive constituencies. And the larger the class of recipients, the greater the pressure for accelerated increases. . . . In this situation, where the underlying issue is the deeply emotional one of Church-State relationships, the potential for seriously divisive political consequences needs no elaboration. And while the prospect of such divisiveness may not alone warrant the invalidation of state laws that otherwise survive the careful scrutiny required by the decisions of this Court, it is certainly a "warning signal" not to be ignored.

Our examination of New York's aid provisions, in light of all relevant considerations, compels the judgment that each, as written, has a "primary effect that advances religion" and offends the constitutional prohibition against laws "respecting an establishment of religion."

Mr. Chief Justice BURGER, joined in part by Mr. Justice WHITE, and joined by Mr. Justice REHNQUIST, concurring in part and dissenting in part.

I join in that part of the Court's opinion in *Committee for Public Education and Religious Liberty v. Nyquist*, 413 U. S. 756, which holds the New York "maintenance and repair" provision unconstitutional under the Establishment Clause because it is a direct aid to religion. I disagree, however, with the Court's decisions in *Nyquist* and in *Sloan v. Lemon*, 413 U. S. 825, to strike down the New York and Pennsylanvia tuition grant programs and the New York tax relief provisions. I believe the Court's decisions on those statutory provisions ignore the teachings of *Everson v. Board of Education*, 330 U. S. 1 (1947), and *Board of Education v. Allen*, 392 U. S. 236 (1968), and fail to observe what I thought the Court had held in *Walz v. Tax Comm'n*, 397 U. S. 664 (1970).

While there is no straight line running through our decisions interpreting the Establishment and Free Exercise Clauses of the First Amendment, our cases do, it seems to me, lay down one solid, basic principe: that the Establishment Clause does not forbid governments, state or federal, to enact a program of general welfare under which benefits are distributed to private individuals, even though many of those individuals may elect to use those benefits in ways that "aid" religious instruction or worship.

The essence of all these decisions, I suggest, is that government aid to individuals generally stands on an entirely different footing from direct aid to religious institutions. I say "generally" because it is obviously possible to conjure hypothetical statutes that constitute either a subterfuge for direct aid to religious institutions or a discriminatory enactment favoring religious over nonreligious activities.... But, at least where the state law is genuinely directed at enhancing a recognized freedom of individuals, even one involving both secular and religious consequences, such as the rights of parents to send their children to private schools . . . the Establishment Clause no longer has a prohibitive effect.

The answer, I believe, lies in the experienced judgment of various members of this Court over the years that the balance between the policies of free exercise and establishment of religion tips in favor of the former when the legislation moves away from direct aid to religious institutions and takes on the character of general aid to individual families. This judgment reflects the caution with which we scrutinize any effort to give official support to religion and the tolerance with which we treat general welfare legislation. But, whatever its basis, that principle is established in our cases, from the early case of *Quick Bear* to the more recent holdings in *Everson* and *Allen*, and it ought to be followed here.

The only discernible difference between the programs in *Everson* and *Allen* and these cases is in the method of the distribution of benefits: here the particular benefits of the Pennsylvania and New York statutes are given only to parents of private-school children, while in *Everson* and *Allen* the statutory benefits were made available to parents of both public- and private-school children. But to regard that difference as constitutionally meaningful is to exalt form over substance. It is beyond dispute that the parents of public-school children in New York and Pennsylvania presently receive the "benefit" of having their children educated totally at state expense; the statutes enacted in those States and at issue here merely attempt to equalize that "benefit" by giving to parents of private-school children, in the form of dollars or tax deductions, what the parents of public-school children receive in kind. It is no more than simple equity to grant partial relief to parents who support the public schools they do not use.

Since I am unable to discern in the Court's analysis of *Everson* and *Allen* any neutral principle to explain the result reached in these cases, I fear that the Court has in reality followed the unsupportable approach of measuring the "effect" of a law by the percentage of the recipients who choose to use the money for religious, rather than secular, education.

With all due respect, I submit that such a consideration is irrelevant to a constitutional determination of the "effect" of a statute. For purposes of constitutional adjudication of that issue, it should make no difference whether 5%, 20%, or 80% of the beneficiaries of an educational program of general application elect to utilize their benefits for religious purposes. The "primary effect" branch of our three-pronged test was never, at least to my understanding, intended to vary with the *number* of churches benefited by a statute under which state aid is distributed to private citizens.

Such a consideration, it is true, might be relevant in ascertaining whether the *primary legislative purpose* was to advance the cause of religion. But the Court has, and I think correctly, summarily dismissed the contention that either New York of Pennsylvania had an improper purpose in enacting these laws.

Mr. Justice REHNQUIST, with whom THE CHIEF JUSTICE and Mr. Justice WHITE concur, dissenting in part.

The opinions in *Walz* . . . make it clear that tax deducations and exemptions, even when directed to religious institutions, occupy quite a different constitutional status under the Religion Clauses of the First Amendment than do outright grants to such institutions.

. . . the deduction here allowed is analytically no different from any other flat-rate exemptions or deductions currently in use in both federal and state tax systems. Surely neither the standard deducation, usable by those taxpayers who do not itemize their deducations, nor personal or dependency exemptions, for example, bear any relationship whatsoever to the actual expenses accrued in earning any of them. Yet none of these could properly be called a reimbursement from the State.

The sole difference between the flat-rate exemptions currently in widespread use and the deduction established in §§ 4 and 5 is that the latter provides a regressive benefit. This legislative judgment, however, as to the appropriate spread of the expense of public and nonpublic education is consonant with the State's concern that those at the lower end of the income brackets are less able to exercise freely their consciences by sending their children to nonpublic schools, and is surely consistent with the "benevolent neutrality" we try to uphold in reconciling the tension between the Free Exercise and Establishment Clauses.

Both *Everson* and *Allen* gave significant recognition to the "benevolent neutrality" concept, and the Court was guided by the fact that any effect from state aid to parents has a necessarily attenuated impact on religious institutions when compared to direct aid to such institutions.

The reimbursement and tax benefit plans today struck down, no less than the plans in *Everson* and *Allen*, are consistent with the principle of neutrality. . . . the impact, if any, on religious education from the aid granted is significantly diminished by the fact that the benefits go to the parents rather than to the institutions.

The increasing difficulties faced by private schools in our country are no reason at all for this Court to readjust the admittedly rough-hewn limits on governmental involvement with religion which are found in the First and Fourteenth Amendments. But, quite understandably, these difficulties can be expected to lead to efforts on the part of those who wish to keep alive pluralism in education to obtain through legislative channels forms of permissible public assistance which were not thought necessary a generation ago. Within the limits permitted by the Constitution, these decisions are quite rightly hammered out on the legislative anvil. If the Constitution does indeed allow for play in the legislative joints . . . the Court must distinguish between a new exercise of power within constitutional limits and an exercise of legislative power which transgresses those limits. I believe the Court has failed to make that distinction here, and I therefore dissent.

Mr. Justice WHITE, joined in part by THE CHIEF JUSTICE and Mr. Justice REHNQUIST, dissenting.

Each of the States regards the education of its young to be a critical matter — so much so that it compels school attendance and provides an educational system at public expense. Any otherwise qualified child is entitled to a free elementary and secondary school education, or at least an education that costs him very little as compared with its cost to the State.

This Court has held, however, that the Due Process Clause of the Fourteenth Amendment to the Constitution entitles parents to send their children to nonpublic schools, secular or sectarian, if those schools are sufficiently competent to educate the child in the necessary secular subjects.... About 10% of the Nation's children, approximately 5.2 million students, now take this option and are not being educated in public schools at public expense. Under state law these children have a right to a free public education and it would not appear unreasonable if the State, relieved of the expense of educating a child in the public school, contributed to the expense of his education elsewhere. The parents of such children pay taxes, including school taxes. They could receive in return a free education in the public schools. They prefer to send their children, as they have the right to do, to nonpublic schools that furnish the satsifactory equivalent of a public school education but also offer subjects or other assumed advantages not available in public schools. Constitutional considerations aside, it would be understandable if a State gave such parents a call on the public treasury up to the amount it would have cost the State to educate the child in public school, or, to put it another way, up to the amount the parents save the State by not sending their children to public school.

In light of the Free Exercise Clause of the First Amendment, this would seem particularly the case where the parent desires his child to attend a school that offers not only secular subjects but religious training as well. A State should put no unnecessary obstacles in the way of religious training for the young.

The dimensions of the situation are not difficult to outline. The 5.2 million private elementary and secondary school students in 1972 attended some 3,200 nonsectarian private schools and some 18,000 schools that are church related. Twelve thousand of the latter were Roman Catholic schools and enrolled 4.37 million pupils or 83% of the total nonpublic school membership. Sixty-two percent of nonpublic school students are concentrated in eight industrialized, urbanized States . . . Eighty-three percent of the nonpublic school enrollment is to be found in large metropolitan areas. Nearly one out of five students in cities that are among the Nation's largest is enrolled in a nonpublic school.

Nonpublic school enrollment has dropped at the rate of 6% per year for the past five years. Projected to 1980, it is estimated that seven States . . . will lose 1,416,122 nonpublic school students. Whatever the reasons, there has been, and there probably will continue to be, a movement to the public schools, with the prospect of substantial increases in public school budgets that are already under intense attack and with the States and cities that are primarily involved already facing severe financial crises. It is this prospect that has prompted some of these States to attempt, by a variety of devices, to save, or slow the demise of, the nonpublic school system, an educational resource that could deliver quality education at a cost to the public substantially below the per-pupil cost of the public schools.

I am quite unreconciled to the Court's decision in *Lemon v. Kurtzman* . . . I . . . have little difficulty in accepting the New York maintenance grant, which does not and could not, by its terms, approach the actual repair and maintenance cost incurred in connection with the secular education services performed for the

State in parochial schools. But, accepting *Lemon* and the invalidation of the New York maintenance grant, I would, with THE CHIEF JUSTICE and Mr. Justice REHNQUIST, sustain the New York and Pennsylvania tuition grant statutes and the New York tax credit provisions.

There is no doubt here that Pennsylvania and New York have sought in the challenged laws to keep their parochial schools system alive and capable of providing adequate secular education to substantial numbers of students. This purpose satisfies the Court, even though to rescue schools that would otherwise fail will inevitably enable those schools to continue whatever religious functions they perform. By the same token, it seems to me, preserving the secular functions of these schools is the overriding consequence of these laws and the resulting, but incidental, benefit to religion should not invalidate them.

SLOAN v. LEMON.

CROUTER v. LEMON.

413 U. S. 825

Decided June 25, 1973 — three Justices dissenting.

Mr. Justice POWELL delivered the opinion of the Court.

On June 28, 1971, this Court handed down *Lemon v. Kurtzman*, 403 U. S. 602, in which Pennsylvania's "Nonpublic Elementary and Secondary Education Act" was held unconstitutional as violative of the Establishment Clause of the First Amendment.

On August 27, 1971, the Pennsylvania General Assembly promulgated a new aid law, entitled the "Parent Reimbursement Act for Nonpublic Education," providing funds to reimburse parents for a portion of tuition expenses incurred in sending their children to nonpublic schools. Shortly thereafter, this suit, challenging the enactment and seeking declaratory and injunctive relief, was filed in the United States District Court for the Eastern District of Pennsylvania.

We have today held in *Committee for Public Education and Religious Liberty v. Nyquist*, 413 U. S. 756, that New York's tuition reimbursement legislation has the impermissible effect of advancing religious institutions and is therefore unconstitutional under the Establishment Clause. Because we find no constitutionally significant difference between New York's and Pennsylvania's programs, that decision compels our affirmance of the District Court's decision here.

Pennsylvania's "Parent Reimbursement Act for Nonpublic Education" provides for reimbursement to parents who pay tuition for their children to attend the State's nonpublic elementary and secondary schools. . . . The money to fund this program is to be derived from a portion of the revenues from the State's tax on cigarette sales, and is to be administered by a five-member committee appointed by the Governor, known as the "Pennsylvania Parent Assistance Authority." In an effort to avoid the "entanglement" problem that flawed its prior aid statute, *Lemon v. Kurtzman* . . . the new legislation specifically precludes the administering authority from having any "direction, supervision or control over the policy determinations, personnel, curriculum, program of instruction or any other aspect of the administration or operation of any nonpublic school or schools." Similarly, the statute imposes no restrictions or limitations on the uses to which the reimbursement allotments can be put by the qualifying parents.

. Like the New York tuition program, the Pennsylvania law is prefaced by "legislative findings," which emphasize its underlying secular purposes: parents who send their children to nonpublic schools reduce the total cost of public education; "inflation, plus sharply rising costs of education, now combine to place in jeopardy the ability of such parents fully to carry this burden"; if the State's 500,000 nonpublic school children were to transfer to the public schools, the annual operating costs to the State would be $400 million, and the added capital costs would exceed $1 billion; therefore, "parents who maintain students in nonpublic schools provide a vital service" and deserve at least partial reimbursement for alleviating an otherwise "intolerable public burden." We certainly do not question now, any more than we did two Terms ago in *Lemon v. Kurtzman*, the reality and legitimacy of Pennsylvania's secular purposes.

For purposes of determining whether the Pennsylvania tuition reimbursement program has the impermissible effect of advancing religion, we find no constitutionally significant distinctions between this law and the one declared invalid today in *Nyquist*.

The State has singled out a class of its citizens for a special economic benefit. Whether that benefit be viewed as a simple tuition subsidy, as an incentive to parents to send their children to sectarian schools, or as a reward for having done so, at bottom its intended consequences is to preserve and support religion-oriented institutions. We think it plain that this is quite unlike the sort of "indirect" and "incidental" benefits that flowed to sectaian schools from programs aiding *all* parents by supplying bus transportation and secular textbooks for their children. Such benefits were carefully restricted to the purely secular side of church-affiliated institutions and provided no special aid for those who had chosen to support religious schools. Yet such aid approached the "verge" of the constitutionally impermissible.

Appellants ask this Court to declare the provisions severable and thereby to allow tuition reimbursement for parents of children attending schools that are not church related. . . . we have been shown no reason to upset the District Court's conclusion that aid to the nonsectarian school could not be severed from aid to the sectarian. The statute nowhere sets up this suggested dichotomy between sectarian and nonsectarian schools, and to approve such a distinction here would be to create a program quite different from the one the legislature actually adopted. . . . Even if the Act were clearly severable, valid aid to nonpublic, nonsectarian schools would . provide no lever for aid to their sectarian counterparts.

In holding today that Pennsylvania's post-*Lemon v. Kurtzman* attempt to avoid the Establishment Clause's prohibition against government entanglements with religion has failed to satisfy the parallel bar against laws having a primary effect that advances religion, we are not unaware that appellants and those who have endeavored to formulate systems of state aid to nonpublic education may feel that the decisions of this Court have, indeed, presented them with the "insoluble paradox" to which Mr. Justice White referred in his separate opinion in *Lemon v. Kurtzman* . . . But if novel forms of aid have not readily been sustained by this Court, the "fault" lies not with the doctrines which are said to create a paradox but rather with the Establishment Clause itself: "Congress" and the States by virtue of the Fourteenth Amendment "shall make no law respecting an establishment of religion." With that judgment we are not free to tamper, and while there is "room for play in the joints," . . . the Amendment's proscription clearly forecloses Pennsylvania's tuition reimbursement program.

WHEELER v. BARRERA.

417 U. S. 402

Decided June 10, 1974 — one Justice dissenting.

Mr. Justice BLACKMUN delivered the opinion of the Court.

Title I of the Elementary and Secondary Education Act of 1965, as amended . . provides for federal funding of special programs for educationally deprived children in both public and private schools.

This suit was instituted on behalf of parochial school students who were eligible for Title I benefits and who claimed that the public school authorities in their area, in violation of the Act, failed to provide adequate Title I programs for private school children as compared with those programs provided for public school children. The defendants answered that the extensive aid sought by the plaintiffs exceeded the requirements of Title I and contravened the State's Constitution and state law and public policy. First Amendment rights were also raised by the parties.

Title I is the first federal-aid-to-education program authorizing assistance for private school children as well as for public school children. The Congress, by its statutory declaration of policy and otherwise, recognized that all children from educationally deprived areas do not necessarily attend the public schools, and that, since the legislative aim was to provide needed assistance to educationally deprived *children* rather than to specific schools, it was necessary to include eligible private school children among the beneficiaries of the Act.

Since the Act was designed to be administered by local *public* education officials, a number of problems naturally arise in the delivery of services to eligible private school pupils.

The questions that arise in this case concern the scope of the State's duty to insure that a program submitted by a local agency under Title I provides "comparable" services for eligible private school children.

In this Court the parties are at odds over two issues: First, whether on this record Title I requires the assignment of publicly employed teachers to provide remedial instruction during regular school hours on the premises of private schools attended by Title I eligible students, and second, whether that requirement, if it exists, contravenes the First Amendment. We conclude that we cannot reach and decide either issue at this stage of the proceedings.

At the outset, we believe that the Court of Appeals erred in holding that federal law governed the question whether on-the-premises private school instruction is permissible under Missouri law. Whatever the case might be if there were no expression of specific congressional intent, Title I evinces a clear intention that state constitutional spending proscriptions not be pre-empted as a condition of accepting federal funds. The key issue, namely, whether federal aid is money "donated to any state fund for public school purposes," within the meaning of the Missouri Constitution . . . is purely a question of state and not federal law. By characterizing the problem as one involving "federal" and not "state" funds, and then concluding that federal law governs, the Court of Appeals, we feel, in effect nullified the Act's policy of accommodating state law. The correct rule is that the "federal law" under Title I is to the effect that state law should not be disturbed.

Furthermore, in the present posture of this case, it was unnecessary for the federal court even to reach the issue whether on-the-premises parochial school instruction is permissible under state law. . . . the State is not obligated by Title I to provide on-the-premises instruction. The mandate is to provide "comparable" services.

The Court of Appeals properly recognized, as we have noted, that petitioners failed to meet their broad obligation and commitment under the Act to provide comparable programs. "Comparable," however, does not mean "identical," and, contrary to the assertions of both sides, we do not read the Court of Appeals' opinion or, for that matter, the Act itself, as ever requiring that identical services be provided in nonpublic schools.

Inasmuch as comparable, and not identical, services are required, the mere fact that public school children are provided on-the-premises Title I instruction does not necessarily create an obligation to make identical provision for private school children. Congress expressly recognized that different and unique problems and needs might make it appropriate to utilize different programs in the private schools. A requirement of identity would run directly counter to this recognition.

In essence, respondents are asking this Court to hold, as a matter of federal law, that one mode of delivering remedial Title I services is superior to others. To place on this Court, or on any federal court, the responsibility of ruling on the relative merits of various possible Title I programs seriously misreads the clear intent of Congress to leave decisions of that kind to the local and state agencies. It is unthinkable, both in terms of the legislative history and the basic structure of the federal judiciary, that the courts be given the function of measuring the comparative desirability of various pedagogical methods contemplated by the Act.

Of course, the cooperation and assistance of the officials of the private school is obviously expected and required in order to design a program that is suitable for the private school. It is clear, however, that the Act places ultimate responsibility and control with the public agency, and the overall program is not to be defeated simply because the private school refuses to participate unless the aid is offered in the particular form it requests. The private school may refuse to participate if the local program does not meet with its approval. But the result of this would then be that the private school's eligible children, the direct and intended beneficiaries of the Act, would lose. The Act, however, does not give the private school a veto power over the program selected by the local agency.

In sum, although it may be difficult, it is not impossible under the Act to devise and implement a legal local Title I program with comparable services despite the use of on-the-premises instruction in the public schools but not in the private schools.

The second major issue is whether the Establishment Clause of the First Amendment prohibits Missouri from sending public school teachers paid with Title I funds into parochial schools to teach remedial course. . . . it is possible for the petitioners to comply with Title I without utilizing on-the-premises parochial school instruction. Moreover, even if, on remand, the state and local agencies do exercise their discretion in favor of such instruction, the range of possibilities is a broad one and the First Amendment implications may vary according to the precise contours of the plan that is formulated. For example, a program whereby a former parochial school teacher is paid with Title I funds to teach full-time in a parochial school undoubtedly would present quite different problems than if a public school teacher, solely under public control, is sent into a parochial school to teach special remedial courses a few hours a week. At this time we intimate no view as to the Establishment Clause effect of any particular program.

It would be wholly inappropriate for us to attempt to render an opinion on the First Amendment issue when no specific plan is before us. A federal court does not sit to render a decision on hypothetical facts, and the Court of Appeals was correct in so concluding.

Under the Act, respondents are entitled to comparable services, and they are, therefore, entitled to relief. As we have stated repeatedly herein, they are not entitled to any particular form of service, and it is the role of the state and local agencies, and not of the federal courts, at least at this stage, to formulate a suitable plan.

Mr. Justice WHITE, concurring in the judgment.

The Court intimates no opinion as to whether using federal funds to pay teachers giving special instruction on private school premises would be constitutional. It suggests, however, that there may be other ways of satisfying the comparability requirement that the State should consider; and unless the State is being asked to chase rainbows, it is inferred that there are programs and services comparable to on-the-premises instruction that the State could furnish private schools without violating the First Amendment. I would have thought that any such arrangement would be impermissible under the Court's recent cases construing the Establishment Clause. Not having joined those opinions, I am pleasantly surprised by what appears to be a suggestion that federal funds may in some respects be used to finance sectarian instruction of students in private elementary and secondary schools. If this is the case, I suggest that the Court should say so expressly. Failing that, however, I concur in the judgment.

Mr. Justice DOUGLAS, dissenting.

The case comes to us in an attractive posture, as the Act of Congress is in terms aimed to help "educationally deprived" children, whether they are in public or parochial schools, and I fear the judiciary has been seduced. But we must remember that "the propriety of the legislature's purposes may not immunize from further scrutiny a law which either has a primary effect that advances religion, or which fosters excessive entanglements between Church and State."

All education in essence is aimed to help children, whether bright or retarded. Schools do not exist — whether public or parochial — to keep teachers employed.

. . . the First Amendment says "Congress shall make no law respecting an establishment of religion." In common understanding there is no surer way of "establishing" an institution than by financing it.

Parochial schools are tied to the proclamation and inculcation of a particular religious faith — sometimes Catholic, sometimes Presbyterian, sometimes Anglican, sometimes Lutheran, and so on.

The emanations from the Court's opinion are, as suggested by Justice WHITE, at war with our prior decisions. Federal financing of an apparently nonsectarian aspect of parochial school activities, if allowed, is not even a subtle evasion of First Amendment prohibitions. The parochial school is a unit; its budget is a unit; pouring in federal funds for what seems to be a nonsectarian phase of parochial school activities "establishes" the school so that in effect, if not in purpose, it becomes stronger financially and better able to proselytize its particular faith by having more funds left over for that objective. Allowing the State to finance the secular part of a sectarian school's program "makes a grave constitutional decision turn merely on cost accounting and bookkeeping entries."

The present case is plainly not moot; a case of controversy exists; and it is clear that if the traditional First Amendment barriers are to be maintained, no program serving students in parochal schools could be designed under this Act — whether regular school hours are used, or after-school hours, or weekend hours. The plain truth is that under the First Amendment, as construed to this day, the Act is unconstitutional to the extent it supports sectarian schools, whether directly or through its students.

We should say so now, and save the endless hours and efforts which hopeful people will expend in an effort to constitutionalize what is impossible without a constitutional amendment.

MEEK v. PITTINGER.

421 U. S. 349

Decided May 19, 1975 — three dissenting opinions.

Mr. Justice STEWART announced the judgment of the Court . . .

With the stated purpose of assuring that every schoolchild in the Commonwealth will equitably share in the benefits of auxiliary services, textbooks, and instructional material provided free of charge to children attending public schools, the Pennsylvania General Assembly in 1972 added Acts 194 and 195 . . . to the Pennsylvania Public School Code of 1949 . . .

Act 194 authorizes the Commonwealth to provide "auxiliary services" to all children enrolled in nonpublic elementary and secondary schools meeting Pennsylvania's compulsory attendance requirements. "Auxiliary services" include counseling, testing, and psychological services, speech and hearing therapy, teaching and related services for exceptional children, for remedial students, and for the educationally disadvantaged, "and such other secular, neutral, nonideological services as are of benefit to nonpublic school children and are presently or hereafter provided for public school children of the Commonwealth." Act 194 specifies that the teaching and services are to be provided in the nonpublic schools themselves by personnel drawn from the appropriate "intermediate unit," part of the public school system of the Commonwealth established to provide special services to local school districts.

Act 195 authorizes the State Secretary of Education, either directly or through the intermediate units, to lend textbooks without charge to children attending nonpublic elementary and secondary schools that meet the Commonwealth's compulsory attendance requirements.

Act 195 also authorizes the Secretary of Education, pursuant to requests from the appropriate nonpublic school officials, to lend directly to the nonpublic schools "instructional materials and equipment, useful to the education" of nonpublic schoolchildren. "Instructional materials" are defined to include periodicals, photographs, maps, charts, sound recordings, films, "or any other printed and published materials of a similar nature." "Instructional equipment," as defined by the Act, includes projection equipment, recording equipment, and laboratory equipment.

Primary among the evils against which the Establishment Clause protects "have been 'sponsorship, financial support, and active involvement of the soverign in religious activities.'. . ." The Court has broadly stated that "[n]o tax in any amount, large or small, can be levied to support any religious activities or institutions, whatever they may be called, or whatever form they may adopt to teach or practice religion.". . . But it is clear that not all legislative programs that provide indirect or incidental benefit to a religious institution are prohibited by the Constitution. . . . "The problem, like many problems in constitutional law, is one of degree."

The District Court held that the textbook loan provisions of Act 195 are constitutionally indistinguishable from the New York textbook loan program upheld in *Board of Education v. Allen*, 392 U. S. 236. We agree.

Like the New York program, the textbook provisions of Act 195 extend to all schoolchildren the benefits of Pennsylvania's well-established policy of lending textbooks free of charge to elementary and secondary school students.... Thus, the financial benefit of Pennsylvania's textbook program, like New York's, is to parents and children, not to the nonpublic schools.

In sum, the textbook loan provisions of Act 195 are in every material respect identical to the loan program approved in *Allen*.

Although textbooks are lent only to students, Act 195 authorizes the loan of instructional material and equipment directly to qualifying nonpublic elementary and secondary schools in the Commonwealth. The appellants assert that such direct aid to Pennsylvania's nonpublic schools, including church-related institutions, constitutes an impermissible establishment of religion.

Act 195 is accompanied by legislative findings that the welfare of the Commonwealth requires that present and future generations of schoolchildren be assured ample opportunity to develop their intellectual capacities. ... We accept the legitimacy of this secular legislative purpose.... But we agree with the appellants that the direct loan of instructional material and equipment has the unconstitutional primary effect of advancing religion because of the predominantly religious character of the schools benefiting from the Act.

The only requirement imposed on nonpublic schools to qualify for loans of instructional material and equipment is that they satisfy the Commonwealth's compulsory attendance law by providing, in the English language, the subjects and activities prescribed by the standards of the State Board of Education.... In fact, of the 1,320 nonpublic schools in Pennsylvania that comply with the requirements of the compulsory attendance law and thus qualify for aid under Act 195, more than 75% are church-related or religiously affiliated educational institutions. Thus, the primary beneficiaries of Act 195's instructional material and equipment loan provisions, like the beneficiaries of the "secular educational services" reimbursement program considered in *Lemon v. Kurtzman*, and the parent tuition reimbursement plan considered in *Sloan v. Lemon*, are nonpublic schools with a predominant sectarian character.

The church-related elementary and secondary schools that are the primary beneficiaries of Act 195's instructional material and equipment loans typify ... religion-pervasive institutions. The very purpose of many of those schools is to provide an integrated secular and religious education; the teaching process is, to a large extent, devoted to the inculcation of religious values and belief. ... Substantial aid to the educational function of such schools, accordingly, necessarily results in aid to the sectarian school enterprise as a whole. ... For this reason, Act 195's direct aid to Pennsylvania's predominantly church-related, nonpublic elementary and secondary schools, even though ostensibly limited to wholly neutral, secular instructional material and equipment, inescapably results in the direct and substantial advancement of religious activity ... and thus constitutes an impermissible establishment of religion.

Unlike Act 195, which provides only for the loan of teaching material and equipment, Act 194 authorizes the Secretary of Education, through the intermediate units, to supply professional staff, as well as supportive materials, equipment, and personnel, to the nonpublic schools of the Commonwealth. The "auxiliary services" authorized by Act 194 — remedial and accelerated instruction, guidance counseling and testing, and speech and hearing services — are provided directly to nonpublic schoolchildren with the appropriate special need. But the services are provided only on the nonpublic school premises, and only when "requested by nonpublic school representatives."

The legislative findings accompanying Act 194 are virtually identical to those in Act 195 . . .

That Act 194 authorizes state-funding of teachers only for remedial and exceptional students, and not for normal students participating in the core curriculum, does not distinguish this case from *Earley v. DiCenso* and *Lemon v. Kurtzman* . . . Whether the subject is "remedial reading," "advanced reading," or simply "reading," a teacher remains a teacher, and the danger that religious doctrine will become intertwined with secular instruction persists.

The fact that the teachers and counselors providing auxiliary serivces are employees of the public intermediate unit, rather than of the church-related schools in which they work, does not substantially eliminate the need for continuing surveillance. To be sure, auxiliary services personnel, because not employed by the nonpublic schools, are not directly subject to the discipline of a religious authority. . . . But they are performing important educational services in schools in which education is an integral part of the dominant sectarian mission and in which an atmosphere dedicated to the advancement of religious belief is constantly maintained. . . . To be certain that auxiliary teachers remain religiously neutral, as the Constitution demands, the State would have to impose limitations on the activities of auxiliary personnel and then engage in some form of continuing surveillance to ensure that those restrictions were being followed.

The recurrent nature of the appropriation process guarantees annual reconsideration of Act 194 and the prospect of repeated confrontation between proponents and opponents of the auxiliary services program. The Act thus provides successive opportunities for political fragmentation and division along religious lines, one of the principal evils against which the Establishment Clause was intended to protect. . . . This potential for political entanglement, together with the administrative entanglement which would be necessary to ensure that auxiliary services personnel remain strictly neutral and nonideological when functioning in church-related schools, compels the conclusion that Act 194 violates the constitutional prohibition against laws "respecting an establishment of religion."

Mr. Justice BRENNAN, with whom Mr. Justice DOUGLAS and Mr. Justice MARSHALL join, concurring and dissenting.

I join in the reversal of the District Court's judgment insofar as that judgment upheld the constitutionality of Act 194 and the provisions of Act 195 respecting instructional materials and equipment, but dissent from . . . the affirmance of the judgment upholding the constitutionality of the textbook provisions of Act 195.

A three-factor test by which to determine the compatability with the

Establishment Clause of state subsidies of sectarian educational institutions has evolved over 50 years of this Court's stewardship in the field. The law in question must, first, reflect a clearly secular legislative purpose, second, have a primary effect that neither advances nor inhibits religion, and, third, avoid excessive government entanglement with religion. But four years ago, the Court, albeit without express recognition of the fact, added a significant fourth factor to the test: "A broader base of entanglement of yet a different character is presented by the divisive political potential of these state programs." *Lemon v. Kurtzman,* 403 U. S. 602, 622 (1971).

Contrary to the plain and explicit teaching of *Kurtzman* and *Nyquist,* however, and inconsistently with its own treatment of Act 194, the Court, in considering the constitutionality of Act 195 says not a single word about the political divisiveness factor . . . of the opinion upholding the textbook loan program created by that Act . . .

. . . *Allen,* which I joined, was decided before *Kurtzman* ordained that the political divisiveness factor must be involved in the weighing process, and understandably neither the parties to *Allen* nor the Court addressed that factor in that case. But whether or not *Allen* can withstand overruling in the light of *Kurtzman* and *Nyquist,* which I question, it is clear that *Kurtzman* — which, I repeat, applied the factor to a Pennsylvania program that included reimbursement for the cost of textbooks — requires that the Court weigh the factor in the instant case. Further, giving the factor the weight that *Kurtzman* and *Nyquist* require, compels, in my view the conclusion that the textbook loan program of Act 195, equally with the program for loan of instructional materials and equipment, violates the Establishment Clause.

First, it is pure fantasy to treat the textbook program as a loan to students. . . . the regulations implementing Act 195 make clear, as the record in *Allen* did not, that the nonpublic school in Pennsylvania is something more than a conduit between the State and pupil. The Commonwealth has promulgated "Guidelines for the Administration of Acts 194 and 195" to implement the statutes. These regulations, unlike those upheld in *Allen,* constitute a much more intrusive and detailed involvement of the State and its processes into the administration of nonpublic schools. . . . The guidelines make crystal clear that the nonpublic school, not its pupils, is the motivating force behind the textbook loan, and that virtually the entire loan transaction is to be, and is in fact, conducted between officials of the nonpublic school, on the one hand, and officers of the state, on the other.

Second, in any event, *Allen* itself made clear that, far from providing a *per se* immunity from examination of the substance of the State's program, even if the fact were, and it is not, that textbooks are loaned to the children rather than to the schools, that is only one among the factors to be weighed in determining the compatibility of the program with the Establishment Clause. . . . And, clearly, in the context of application of the factor of political divisiveness, it is wholly irrelevant whether the loan is to the children or to the school. A divisive political potential exists because aid programs, like Act 195, are dependent on continuing annual appropriations, and Act 195's textbook loan program, even if we accept it as a form of loans to students, involves increasingly massive sums now approaching $5,000,000 annually. It would blind reality to treat massive aid to nonpublic schools, under the guise of loans to the students, as not creating "a serious potential for divisive conflict over the issue of aid to religion."

Finally, the textbook loan provisions of Act 195, even if ostensibly limiting loans to nonpublic school children, violate the Establishment Clause for reasons independent of the political divisiveness factor. As I have said, unlike the New York statute in *Allen* which extended assistance to all students, whether attending public or nonpublic schools, Act 195 extends textbook assistance only to a special class of students, children who attend nonpublic schools which are, as the Court notes, primarily religiously oriented. The Act in that respect contains the same fatal defect as the New Jersey statute held violative of the Establishment Clause in *Public Funds v. Marburger* . . . 417 U. S. 961 (1947) . . . *Marburger* thus establishes that the Court's reliance today upon *Allen* is clearly misplaced.

Indeed, that reliance is also misplaced in light of its own holding today invalidating the provisions of Act 195 respecting the loan of instructional materials and equipment. I have no doubt that such materials and equipment are tools that substantially enhance the quality of the secular education provided by the religiously oriented schools. But surely the heart-tools of that education are the textbooks that are prescribed for use and kept at the schools, albeit formally at the request of the students. Thus, what the Court says of the instructional materials and equipment . . . may be said perhaps even more accurately of the textbooks . . .

Mr. Chief Justice BURGER, concurring in the judgment in part and dissenting in part.

I agree with the Court only insofar as it affirms the judgment of the District Court. My limited agreement with the Court as to this action leads me, however, to agree generally with the views expressed by Mr. Justice REHNQUIST and Mr. Justice WHITE in regard to the other programs under review. I especially find it difficult to accept the Court's extravagant suggestion of potential entanglement which it finds in the "auxiliary services" program of . . . 194. Here, the Court's holding, it seems to me, goes beyond any prior holdings of this Court and, indeed, conflicts with our holdings in *Board of Education v. Allen* . . . and *Lemon v. Kurtzman* . . . There is absolutely no support in this record or, for that matter, in ordinary human experience to support the concern some see with respect to the "dangers" lurking in extending common, nonsectarian tools of the education process — especially remedial tools — to students in private schools. . . . Certainly, there is no basis in "experience and history" to conclude that a State's attempt to provide — through the services of its own state-selected professionals — the remedial assistance necessary for *all* its children poses the same potential for unnecessary administrative entanglement or divisive political confrontation which concerned the Court in *Lemon v. Kurtzman* . . . Indeed, I see at least as much potential for divisive political debate in opposition to the crabbed attitude the Court shows in this case.

If the consequence of the Court's holding operated only to penalize *institutions* with a religious affiliation, the result would be grievous enough; nothing in the Religion Clauses of the First Amendment permits governmental power to discriminate *against* or affirmatively stifle religions or religious activity. . . . But this holding does more: it penalizes *children* — children who have the misfortune to have to cope with the learning process under extraordinary heavy physical and psychological burdens, for the most part congenital. This penalty strikes them not because of any act of theirs but because of their parents' choice of religious exercise.

The melancholy consequence of what the Court does today is to force the parent to choose between the "free exercise" of a religious belief by opting for a sectarian education for his child or to forego the opportunity for his child to learn to cope with — or overcome — serious congenital learning handicaps, through remedial assistance financed by his taxes. Affluent parents, by employing private teaching specialists, will be able to cope with this denial of equal protection, which is, for me, a gross violation of Fourteenth Amendment rights, but all others will be forced to make a choice between their judgment as to their children's spiritual needs and their temporal need for special remedial learning assistance.

Mr. Justice REHNQUIST, with whom Mr. Justice WHITE joins, concurring in the judgment in part and dissenting in part.

Substantially for the reasons set forth in my dissent and those of The Chief Justice and Mr. Justice White in *Committee for Public Education & Religious Liberty v. Nyquist* . . . I would affirm the judgment of the District Court.

Act 195 includes a program that provides for the loan of textbooks . . . I agree with the Court that this program is constitutionally indistinguishable from the New York textbook loan program upheld in *Baord of Education v. Allen* . . . and on the authority of that case I join the judgment of the Court insofar as it upholds the textbook loan program.

The Court strikes down other provisions of Act 195 dealing with instructional materials and equipment because it finds that they have "the unconstitutional primary effect of advancing religion because of the predominantly religious character of the schools benefiting from the Act.". . . This apparently follows from the high percentage of nonpublic schools that are "church-related or religiously affiliated educational institutions.". . . I find that approach to the "primary effect" branch of our three-pronged test no more satisfactory in the context of this instructional materials and equipment program than it was in the context of the tuition reimbursement and tax relief programs involved in *Nyquist* . . . and *Sloan* . . .

One need look no further than to the majority opinion for a demonstration of the arbitrariness of the percentage approach to primary effect. In determining the constitutionality of the textbook loan program established by Act 195, the Court views the program in the context of the State's "well-established policy of lending textbooks free of charge to elementary and secondary school students.". . . But when it comes time to consider the same Act's instructional materials and equipment program, which is not alleged to make available to private schools any materials and equipment that are not provided to public schools, the majority strikes down this program because more than 75% of the nonpublic schools are church-related or religiously affiliated.

The failure of the majoirty to justify the differing approaches to textbooks and instructional materials and equipment in the above respect is symptomatic of its failure even to attempt to distinguish the Pennsylvania textbook loan program, which it upholds, from the Pennsylvania instructional materials and equipment loan program, which it finds unconstitutional. . . . I fail to see how the instructional materials and equipment program can be distinguished in any significant respect. Under both programs "ownership remains, at least technically, in the State,". . . Once it is conceded that no danger of diversion exists, it is difficult to articulate any principled basis upon which to distinguish the two Act 195 programs.

As a matter of constitutional law, the holding by the majority that this case is controlled by *Lemon v. Kurtzman* . . . marks a significant *sub silentio* extension of that 1971 decision.

The auxiliary services program established by Act 194 differs from the programs struck down in *Lemon* in two important respects. First the opportunities for religious instruction through the auxiliary services program are greatly reduced because of the considerably more limited reach of the Act.

Even if the distinction between these services and core curricula is thought to be a matter of degree, the second distinction between the programs involved in *Lemon* and Act 194 is a difference in kind. Act 194 provides that these auxiliary services shall be provided by personnel of the *public* school system. Since the danger of entanglement articulated in *Lemon* flowed from the susceptibility of parochial school teachers to "religious control and discipline," I would have assumed that exorcisation of that constitutional "evil" would lead to a different constitutional result. The Court does not contend that the public school employees who would administer the auxiliary services are subject to "religious control and discipline.". . . The decision of the Court that Act 194 is unconstitutional rests ultimately upon the unsubstantiated factual proposition that "[t]he potential for impermissible fostering of religion under these circumstances, although somewhat reduced, is nonetheless present."

I am disturbed as much by the overtones of the Court's opinion as by its actual holding. The Court apparently believes that the Establishment Clause of the First Amendment not only mandates religious neutrality on the part of government but also requires that this Court go further and throw its weight on the side of those who believe that our society as a whole should be a purely secular one. Nothing in the First Amendment or in the cases interpreting it requires such an extreme approach to this difficult question, and "[a]ny interpretation of [the Establishment Clause] and constitutional values it serves must also take account of the free exercise clause and the values it serves."

ROEMER v. BOARD OF PUBLIC WORKS OF MARYLAND.

426 U. S. 736

Decided June 21, 1976 — four Justices dissenting.

Mr. Justice BLACKMUN announced the judgment of the Court . . .

We are asked once again to police the constitutional boundary between church and state. Maryland, this time, is the alleged trespasser. It has enacted a statute which, as amended, provides for annual noncategorical grants to private colleges, among them religiously affiliated institutions, subject only to the restrictions that the funds not be used for "sectarian purposes."

The challenged grant program was instituted by Laws of 1971 . . . provides funding for "any private institution of higher learning within the State of Maryland," provided the institution is accredited by the State Department of Education, was established in Maryland prior to July 1, 1970, maintains one or more "associate of arts or baccalaureate degree" programs, and refrains from awarding "only seminarian or theological degrees.". . . The aid is in the form of an annual fiscal year subsidy to qualifying colleges and universities. The formula by which each institution's entitlement is computed . . . now provides for a qualifying institution to receive, for each full-time student . . . an amount equal to 15% of the State's per full-time pupil appropriation for a student in the state college system. . . . the grants. . . remain noncategorical in nature, and a recipient institution may put them to whatever use it prefers, with but one exception. . . .

> "None of the moneys payable under this subtitle shall be utilized by the institutions for sectarian purposes."

The administration of the grant program is entrusted to the State's Board of Public Works "assisted by the Maryland Council for Higher Education.". . . Primary responsibility for the program rests with the Council of Higher Education, an appointed commission which antedates the aid program . . .

The Council performs what the District Court described as a "two-step screening process" . . . First, it determines whether an institution applying for aid is eligible at all . . . Second, the Council requires that those institutions that are eligible for funds not put them to any sectarian use.

A system of government that makes itself felt as pervasively as ours could hardly be expected never to cross paths with the church. In fact, our State and Federal Governments impose certain burdens upon, and impart certain benefits to, virtually all our activities, and religious activity is not an exception. The Court has enforced a scrupulous neutrality by the State, as among religions, and also as between religious and other activities, but a hermetic separation of the two is an impossibility it has never required.

And religious institutions need not be quarantined from public benefits that are neutrally available to all. . . . The Court has not been blind to the fact that in aiding a religious institution to perform a secular task, the State frees the institution's resources to be put to sectarian ends. If this were impermissible, however, a church could not be protected by the police and fire departments, or have its public sidewalk kept in repair. The Court never has held that religious activities must be discriminated against in this way.

Neutrality is what is required. The State must confine itself to secular objectives, and neither advance nor impede religious activity. Of course, that principle is more easily stated than applied. The Court has taken the view that a secular purpose and a facial neutrality may not be enough, if in fact the State is lending direct support to a religious activity. . . . In *Lemon I* . . . the Court distilled these concerns into a three-prong test, resting in part on prior case law, for the constitutionality of statutes affording aid to church-related schools:

> "First, the statute must have a secular legislative purpose; second, its principal or primary effect must be one that neither advances nor inhibits religion . . . ; finally, the statute must not foster 'an excessive government entanglement with religion.'"

The Court also pointed to another kind of church-state entanglement . . . namely, their "divisive political potential."

So the slate we write on is anything but clean. Instead, there is little room for further refinement of the principles governing public aid to church-affiliated private schools. Our purpose is not to unsettle those principles, so recently reaffirmed . . . or to expand upon them substantially, but merely to insure that they are faithfully applied in this case.

The first part of *Lemon I's* three-part test is not in issue . . . The focus of the debate is on the second and third parts, those concerning the primary effect of advancing religion, and excessive church-state entanglement.

While entanglement is essentially a procedural problem, the primary effect question is the substantive one of what private educational activities, by whatever procedure, may be supported by state funds. *Hunt* requires (1) that no state aid at all go to institutions that are so "pervasively sectarian" that secular activities cannot be separated from sectarian ones, and (2) that if secular activities *can* be separated out, they alone may be funded.

The District Court's finding in this case was that the appellee colleges are not "pervasively sectarian."

It is not our place, however, to reappraise the evidence, unless it plainly fails to support the findings of the trier of facts. That is certainly not the case here, and it would make no difference even if we were to second-guess the District Court in certain particulars. To answer the question whether an institution is so "pervasively sectarian" that it may receive no direct state aid of any kind, it is necessary to paint a general picture of the institution, composed of many elements. The general picture that the District Court has painted of the appellee institutions is similar in almost all respects to that of the church-affiliated colleges considered in *Tilton* and *Hunt*.

Having found that the appellee institutions are not "so permeated by religion that the secular side cannot be separated from the sectarian,". . . the District Court proceeded to the next question posed by *Hunt*: whether aid in fact was extended only to "the secular side." This requirement the court regarded as satisfied by the statutory prohibition against sectarian use, and by the administrative enforcement of that prohibition through the Council for Higher Education. We agree.

If the foregoing answer to the "primary effect" question seems easy, it serves to make the "excessive entanglement" problem more difficult. The statute itself clearly denies the use of public funds for "sectarian purposes." It seeks to avert such use, however, through a process of annual interchange — proposal and approval, expenditure and review — between the colleges and the Council. In answering the question whether this will be an "excessively entangling" relationship, we must consider the several relevant factors identified in prior decisions:

First is the character of the aided institutions. This has been fully described . . . As the District Court found, the colleges perform "essentially secular educational functions,". . . that are distinct and separable from religious activity.

As for the form of aid, we have already noted that no particular use of state funds is before us in this case. The *process* by which aid is disbursed, and a use for it chosen, are before us. We address this as a matter of the "resulting relationship" of secular and religious authority.

As noted, the funding process in an annual one. The subsidies are paid out each year, and they can be put to annually varying uses. The colleges propose particular uses for the Council's approval, and, following expenditure, they report to the Council on the use to which the funds have been put.

We agree with the District Court that "excessive entanglement" does not necessarily result from the fact that the subsidy is an annual one. . . . But if the question is whether this case is more like *Lemon I* or more like *Tilton* — and surely that is the fundamental question before us — the answer must be that it is more like *Tilton*.

The present statute contemplates annual decisions by the Council as to what is a "sectarian purpose," but, as we have noted, the secular and sectarian activities of the colleges are easily separated.

While the form-of-aid distinctions of *Tilton* are thus of questionable importance, the character-of-institution distinctions of *Lemon I* are most impressive. To reiterate a few of the relevant points: the elementary and secondary schooling in *Lemon* came at an impressionable age; the aided schools were "under the general supervision" of the Roman Catholic diocese; each had a local Catholic parish that assumed "ultimate financial responsibility" for it; the principals of the schools were usually appointed by church authorities; religion "pervade[d] the school system"; teachers were specifically instructed by the "Handbook of School Regulations" that "'[r]eligious formation is not confined to formal courses; nor is it restricted to a single subject area.'". . . These things made impossible what is crucial to a nonentangling aid program: the ability of the State to identify and subsidize separate secular functions carried out at the school, without on-the-site inspections being necessary to prevent diversion of the funds to sectarian purposes. The District Court gave primary importance to this consideration, and we cannot say it erred.

As for political divisiveness, the District Court recognized that the annual nature of the subsidy, along with its promise of an increasing demand for state funds as the colleges' dependency grew, aggravated the danger of "[p]olitical fragmentation . . . on religious lines.". . . Nonetheless, the District Court found that the program "does not create a substantial danger of political entanglement."

The District Court's reasoning seems to us entirely sound.

There is no exact science in guaging the entanglement of church and state. The wording of the test, which speaks of "*excessive* entanglement," itself makes that clear. The relevant factors we have identified are to be considered "cumulatively" in judging the degree of entanglement. . . . They may cut different ways, as certainly they do here. In reaching the conclusion that it did, the District Court gave dominant importance to the character of the aided institutions and to its finding that they are capable of separating secular and religious functions. For the reasons stated above, we cannot say that the emphasis was misplaced, or the finding erroneous. The judgment of the District Court is affirmed.

Mr. Justice WHITE, with whom Mr. Justice REHNQUIST joins, concurring in the judgment.

While I join in the judgment of the Court, I am unable to concur in the plurality opinion substantially for the reasons set forth in my opinions in *Lemon v. Kurtzman* . . . and *Committee for Public Education v. Nyquist* . . . I am no more reconciled now to *Lemon I* than I was when it was decided. . . . The threefold test of *Lemon I* imposes unnecessary, and, as I believe today's plurality opinion demonstrates, superfluous tests for establishing "when the State's involvement with religion passes the peril point" for First Amendment purposes.

"It is enough for me that the [State is] financing a separable secular function of overriding importance in order to sustain the legislation here challenged.". . . As long as there is a secular legislative purpose, and as long as the primary effect of the legislation is neither to advance nor inhibit religion, I see no reason — particularly in light of the "sparse language of the Establishment Clause,". . . to take the constitutional inquiry further. . . . However, since 1970, the Court has added a third element to the inquiry: whether there is "an excessive governmental entanglement with religion.". . . I have never understood the constitutional foundation for this added element . . .

Mr. Justice BRENNAN, dissenting.

I agree with Judge Bryan, dissenting from the judgment under review, that the Maryland Act *"in these instances* does in truth offend the Constitution by its provisons of funds, in that it exposes State money for use in advancing religion, no matter the vigilance to avoid it.". . . the Act provides for payment of general subsidies to religious institutions from public funds and I have heretofore expressed my view that "[g]eneral subsidies of religious activities would, of course, constitute impermissible state involvement with religion.". . . This is because general subsidies "tend to promote that type of interdependence between religion and state which the First Amendment was designed to prevent."

Mr. Justice STEWART, dissenting.

The findings in *Tilton* clearly establish that the federal building construction grants benefited academic institutions that made no attempt to inculcate the religious beliefs of the affiliated church. In the present case, by contrast, the compulsory theology courses may be "devoted to deepening religious experiences in the particular faith rather than to teaching theology as an academic discipline.". . . In view of this salient characteristic of the appellee institutions and the noncategorical grants provided to them by the State of Maryland, I agree with the conclusion of the dissenting member of the three-judge court that the challenged Act *"in these instances* does in truth offend the Constitution . . ."

Mr. Justice STEVENS, dissenting.

My views are substantially those expressed by Mr. Justice BRENNAN. However, I would add emphasis to the pernicious tendency of a state subsidy to tempt religious schools to compromise their religious mission without wholly abandoning it. The disease of entanglement may infect a law discouraging wholesome religious activity as well as a law encouraging the propagation of a given faith.

WOLMAN v. WALTER.

433 U. S. 229

Decided June 24, 1977.

Mr. Justice BLACKMUN delivered the opinion of the Court . . .

This is still another case presenting the recurrent issue of the limitations imposed by the Establishment Clause of the First Amendment, made applicable to the States by the Fourteenth Amendment, *Meek v. Pittinger*, 421 U. S. 349, 351 (1975) on state aid to pupils in church-related elementary and secondary schools. Appellants are citizens and taxpayers of Ohio. They challenge all but one of the provisions of Ohio Rev.Code § 3317.06 (Supp.1976) which authorize various forms of aid.

Section 3317.06 was enacted after this Court's May 1975 decision in *Meek v. Pittinger* . . . and obviously is an attempt to conform to the teachings of that decision. . . . In broad outline, the statute authorizes the State to provide nonpublic school pupils with books, instructional materials and equipment, standardized testing and scoring, diagnostic services, therapeutic services, and field trip transportation.

The . . . Funds . . . appropriated are paid to the State's public school districts and are then expended by them. All disbursements made with respect to nonpublic schools have their equivalents in disbursements for public schools, and the amount expended per pupil in nonpublic schools may not exceed the amount expended per pupil in the public schools.

The parties stipulated that, during the 1974-1975 school year there were 720 chartered nonpublic schools in Ohio. Of these, all but 29 were sectarian. More than 96% of the nonpublic enrollment attended sectarian schools, and more than 92% attended Catholic schools. . . . All such schools teach the secular subjects required to meet the State's minimum standards. The state-mandated five-hour day is expanded to include, usually, one-half hour of religious instruction. Pupils who are not members of the Catholic faith are not required to attend religion classes or to participate in religious exercises or activities, and no teacher is required to teach religious doctrine as a part of the secular courses taught in the schools.

The parties also stipulated that nonpublic school officials, if called, would testify that none of the schools covered by the statute discriminate in the admission of pupils or in the hiring of teachers on the basis of race, creed, color, or national origin.

The mode of analysis for Establishment Clause questions is defined by the three-part test that has emerged from the Court's decisions. In order to pass muster, a statute must have a secular legislative purpose, must have a principal or primary effect that neither advances nor inhibits reilgion, and must not foster an excessive government entanglement with religion.

In the present case we have no difficulty with the first prong of this three-part test. We are satisfied that the challenged statute reflects Ohio's legitimate interest in protecting the health of its youth and in providing a fertile educational environment for all the school children of the State.

We therefore turn to the task of applying the rules derived from our decisions to the respective provisions of the statute at issue.

Section 3317.06 authorizes the expenditure of funds:

> "(A) To purchase such secular textbooks as have been approved by the superintendent of public instruction for use in public schools in the state and to loan such textbooks to pupils attending nonpublic schools within the district or to their parents. Such loans shall be based upon individual requests submitted by such nonpublic school pupils or parents. . . . As used in this section, 'textbook' means any book or book substitute which a pupil uses as a text or text substitute in a particular class or program in the school he regularly attends."

In addition, it was stipulated:

> "The secular textbooks used in nonpublic schools will be the same as the textbooks used in the public schools of the state. . . .
>
> "Textbooks, including book substitutes, provided under this Act shall be limited to books, reusable workbooks, or manuals, whether bound or in looseleaf form, intended for use as a principal source of study material for a given class or a group of students, a copy of which is expected to be available for the individual use of each pupil in such class or group."

This system for the loan of textbooks to individual students bears a striking resemblance to the systems approved in *Board of Education v. Allen*, 392 U. S. 236 (1968), and in *Meek v. Pittinger* . . . Indeed, the only distinction offered by appellants is that the challenged statute defines "textbook" as "any book or book substitute." Appellants argue that a "book substitute" might include auxiliary equipment and materials that, they assert, may not constitutionally be loaned. . . . We find this argument untenable in light of the statute's separate treatment of instructional materials and equipment . . . and in light of the stipulation defining textbooks as "limited to books, reusable workbooks, or manuals." . . . As read, the statute provides the same protections against abuse as were provided in the textbook programs under consideration in *Allen* and in *Meek*.

. . . we conclude that § 3317.06(A) is constitutional.

Section 3317.06 authorizes expenditure of funds

> "(J) To supply for use by pupils attending nonpublic schools within the district such standardized tests and scoring services as are in use in the public schools of the state."

These tests "are used to measure the progress of students in secular subjects.". . . Nonpublic school personnel are not involved in either the drafting or scoring of the tests. . . . The statute does not authorize any payment to nonpublic school personnel for the costs of administering the tests.

In *Levitt v. Committee for Public Education*, 413 U. S. 472 (1973), this Court invalidated a New York statutory scheme for reimbursement of church-sponsored schools for the expenses of teacher-prepared testing. . . . The system was held unconstitutional because "no means are available, to assure that internally prepared tests are free of religious instruction."

There is no question that the State has a substantial and legitimate interest in insuring that its youth receive an adequate secular education. . . . The State may require that schools that are utilized to fulfill the State's compulsory education requirement meet certain standards of instruction . . . and may examine both teachers and pupils to ensure that the State's legitimate interest is being fulfilled. . . . Under the section at issue, the State provides both the schools and the school district with the means of ensuring that the minimum standards are met. The nonpublic school does not control the content of the test or its result. This serves to prevent the use of the test as a part of religious teaching, and thus avoids that kind of direct aid to religion found present in *Levitt*. Similarly, the inability of the school to control the test eliminates the need for the supervision that gives rise to excessive entanglement. We therefore agree with the District Court's conclusion that § 3317.06(J) is constitutional.

Section 3317.06 authorizes expenditures of funds

> "(D) To provide speech and hearing diagnostic services to pupils attending nonpublic schools within the district. Such service shall be provided in the nonpublic school attended by the pupil receiving the service.
> "(F) To provide diagnostic psychological services to pupils attending nonpublic schools within the district. Such services shall be provided in the school attended by the pupil receiving the service."

It will be observed that these speech and hearing and psychological diagnostic services are to be provided within the nonpublic school. It is stipulated, however, that the personnel . . . who perform the services are employees of the local board of education; that physicians may be hired on a contract basis; that the purpose of these services is to determine the pupil's deficiency or need of assistance; and that treatment of any defect so found would take place off the nonpublic school premises.

Appellants assert that the funding of these services is constitutionally impermissible.

This Court's decisions contain a common thread to the effect that the provision of health services to all school children — public and nonpublic — does not have the primary effect of aiding religion.

In *Meek* the Court did hold unconstitutional a portion of a Pennsylvania statute at issue there that authorized certain auxiliary services — "remedial and accelerated instruction, guidance counseling and testing, speech and hearing services" — on nonpublic school premises. . . . The statute was held unconstitutional on entanglement grounds, namely, that in order to insure that the auxiliary teachers and guidance counselors remained neutral, the State would have to engage in continuing surveillance on the school premises. . . . The Court in *Meek* explicitly stated, however, that the provision of diagnostic speech and hearing services by Pennsylvania seemed "to fall within that class of general welfare services for children that may be provided by the State regardless of the incidental benefit that accrues to church-related schools.". . . The provision of such services was invalidated only because it was found unseverable from the unconstitutional portions of the statute.

The reason for considering diagnostic services to be different from teaching or counseling is readily apparent. First, diagnostic services, unlike teaching or counseling, have little or no educational content and are not closely associated with the educational mission of the nonpublic school. . . . Second, the diagnostician has only limited contact with the child, and that contact involves chiefly the use of objective and professional testing methods to detect students in need of treatment.

We conclude that providing diagnostic services on the nonpublic school premises will not create an impermissible risk of the fostering of ideological views. . . . We therefore hold that §§ 3317.06(D) and (F) are constitutional.

Sections 3317.06(G), (H), (I), and (K) authorize expenditures of funds for certain therapeutic, guidance, and remedial services for students who have been identified as having a need for specialized attention. Personnel providing the services must be employees of the local board of education or under contract with the State Department of Health. The services are to be performed only in public schools, in public centers, or in mobile units located off the nonpublic school premises.

At the outset, we note that in its present posture the case does not properly present any issue concerning the use of a public facility as an adjunct of a sectarian educational enterprise. The District Court construed the statute, as do we, to authorize services only on sites that are "neither physically nor educationally identified with the functions of the nonpublic school.". . . . Thus, the services are to be offered under circumstances that reflect their religious neutrality.

The fact that a unit on a neutral site on occasion may serve only sectarian pupils does not provoke the same concerns that troubled the Court in *Meek*. The influence on a therapist's behavior that is exerted by the fact that he serves a sectarian pupil is qualitatively different from the influence of the pervasive atmosphere of a religious institution. The dangers perceived in *Meek* arose from the nature of the institution, not from the nature of the pupils.

Accordingly, we hold that providing therapeutic and remedial services at a neutral site off the premises of the nonpublic schools will not have the impermissible effect of advancing religion. Neither will there be any excessive entanglement arising from supervision of public employees to insure that they maintain a neutral stance. It can hardly be said that the supervision of public employees performing public functions on public property creates an excessive entanglement between church and state. Sections 3317.06(G), (H), (I), and (K) are constitutional.

Sections 3317.06(B) and (C) authorize expenditures of funds for the purchase and loan to pupils or their parents upon individual request of instructional materials and instructional equipment of the kind in use in the public schools within the district and which is "incapable of diversion to religious use." Section 3317.06 also provides that the materials and equipment may be stored on the premises of a nonpublic school and that publicly hired personnel who administer the lending program may perform their services upon the nonpublic school premises when necessary "for efficient implementation of the lending program."

In *Meek* . . . the Court considered the constitutional validity of a direct loan to nonpublic schools of instructional material and equipment, and, despite the apparent secular nature of the goods, held the loan impermissible.

Appellees seek to avoid *Meek* by emphasizing that it involved a program of direct loans to nonpublic schools. In contrast, the material and equipment at issue under the Ohio statute are loaned to the pupil or his parents. In our view, however, it would exalt form over substance if this distinction were found to justify a result different from that in *Meek*. . . . In view of the impossibility of separating the secular education function from the sectarian, the state aid inevitably flows in part in support of the religious role of the schools.

Accordingly, we hold §§ 3317.06(B) and (C) to be unconstitutional.

Section 3317.06 also authorizes expenditures of funds:

> "(L) To provide such field trip transportation and services to nonpublic school students as are provided to public school students in the district. School districts may contract with commercial transportation companies for such transportation service if school district busses are unavailable."

In *Everson* the Court approved a system under which a New Jersey board of education reimbursed parents for the cost of sending their children to and from school, public or parochial, by public carrier.

The Ohio situation is in sharp contrast. First, the nonpublic school controls the timing of the trips and, within a certain range, their frequency and destinations. Thus, the schools, rather than the children, truly are the recipients of the service and, as this Court has recognized, this fact alone may be sufficient to invalidate the program as impermissible direct aid. . . . Second, although a trip may be to a location that would be of interest to those in public schools, it is the individual teacher who makes a field trip meaningful. . . . The field trips are an integral part of the educational experience, and where the teacher works within and for a sectarian institution, an unacceptable risk of fostering of religion is an inevitable by-product. . . . Funding of field trips . . . must be treated as was the funding of maps and charts in *Meek v. Pittinger* . . . the funding of buildings and tuition in *Committee for Public Education v. Nyquist* . . . and the funding of teacher-prepared tests in *Levitt v. Committee for Public Education*; it must be declared an impermissible direct aid to sectarian education.

We hold § 3317.06(L) to be unconstitutional.

In summary, we hold constitutional those portions of the Ohio statute authorizing the State to provide nonpublic school pupils with books, standardized testing and scoring, diagnostic services, and therapeutic and remedial services.

We hold unconstitutional those portions relating to instructional materials and equipment and field trip services.

Mr. Justice MARSHALL, concurring and dissenting.

The Court upholds the textbook loan provision . . . on the precedent of *Board of Education v. Allen* . . . It also recognizes, however, that there is "a tension" between *Allen* and the reasoning of the Court in *Meek v. Pittinger* . . . I would resolve that tension by overruling *Allen*. I am now convinced that *Allen* is largely responsible for reducing the "high and impregnable" wall between church and state erected by the First Amendment . . . to "a blurred, indistinct, and variable barrier,". . . incapable of performing its vital functions of protecting both church and state.

In *Allen*, we upheld a textbook loan program on the assumption that the sectarian school's twin functions of religious instruction and secular education were separable. . . . In *Meek*, we flatly rejected that assumption as a basis for allowing a State to loan secular teaching materials and equipment to such schools . . . Thus, although *Meek* upheld a textbook loan program on the strength of *Allen*, it left the rationale of *Allen* undamaged only if there is a constitutionally significant difference between a loan of pedagogical materials directly to a sectarian school and a loan of those materials to students for use in sectarian schools. As the Court convincingly demonstrates . . . there is no such difference.

Allen has also been undercut by our recognition in *Lemon* that "the divisive political potential" of programs of aid to sectarian schools is one of the dangers of entanglement of church and state that the First Amendment was intended to forstall.

By overruling *Allen*, we would free ourselves to draw a line between acceptable and unacceptable forms of aid that would be both capable of consistent application and responsive to the concerns discussed above. That line, I believe, should be placed between general welfare programs that serve children in sectarian schools because the schools happen to be a convenient place to reach the programs' target populations and programs of educational assistance. General welfare programs, in contrast to programs of educational assistance, do not provide "[s]ubstantial aid to the educational function" of schools, whether secular or sectarian, and therefore do not provide the kind of assistance to the religious mission of sectarian schools we found impermissible in *Meek*.

Mr. Justice POWELL, concurring in part and dissenting in part.

Our decisions in this troubling area draw lines that often must seem arbitrary. No doubt we could achieve greater analytical tidiness if we were to accept the broadest implications of the observation in *Meek v. Pittinger* . . . that "[s]ubstantial aid to the educational function of [sectarian] schools . . . necessarily results in aid to the sectarian enterprise of a whole." If we took that course, it would become impossible to sustain state aid of any kind — even if the aid is wholly secular in character and is supplied to the pupils rather than the institutions. . . . The persistent desire of a number of States to find proper means of helping sectarian education to survive would be doomed. This Court has not yet thought that such a harsh result is required by the Establishment Clause. Certainly few would consider it in the public interest. Parochial schools, quite apart from their sectarian purpose, have provided an educational alternative for millions of young Americans; they often afford wholesome competition with our public schools; and in some States they relieve substantially the tax burden incident to the operation of public schools.

It is important to keep these issues in perspective. At this point in the 20th century we are quite far removed from the dangers that prompted the Framers to include the Establishment Clause in the Bill of Rights. . . . The risk of significant religious or denominational control over our democratic processes — or even of deep political division along religious lines — is remote, and when viewed against the positive contributions of sectarian schools, any such risk seems entirely tolerable in light of the continuing oversight of this Court.

Mr. Justice STEVENS, concurring in part and dissenting in part.

The line drawn by the Establishment Clause of the First Amendment must also have a fundamental character. It should not differentiate between direct and indirect subsidies, or between instructional materials like globes and maps on the one hand and instructional mateials like textbooks on the other. For that reason, rather than the three-part test described in . . . the Court's opinion, I would adhere to the test enunciated for the Court by Mr. Justice Black:

> "No tax in any amount, large or small, can be levied to support any religious activities or institutions, whatever they may be called, or whatever form they may adopt to teach or practice religion."

Under that test, a state subsidy of sectarian schools is invalid regardless of the form it takes. The financing of buildings, field trips, instructional materials, educational tests, and school books are all equally invalid. For all give aid to the school's educational mission, which at heart is religious. On the other hand, I am not prepared to exclude the possibility that some parts of the statute before us may be administered in a constitutional manner. The State can plainly provide public health services to children attending nonpublic schools. The diagnostic and theraputic services described in . . . the Court's opinion may fall into this category. Although I have some misgivings on this point, I am not prepared to hold this part of the statute invalid on its face.

APPENDIX A

The decisions of the Supreme Court presented in this volume are listed in this Appendix with citation numbers from the *United States Reports*, the *United States Supreme Court Reports, Lawyers' Edition*, and the *Supreme Court Reporter*.

Religion in Public Education

MINERSVILLE SCHOOL DIST. v. GOBITIS. 310 U. S. 586, 84 L ed 1375, 60 S. Ct. 1010, (1940).

WEST VIRGINIA STATE BOARD OF EDUCATION v. BARNETTE. 319 U. S. 624, 87 L ed 1628, 63 S. Ct. 1178, (1943).

McCOLLUM v. BOARD OF EDUCATION OF SCHOOL DIST. NO. 71, CHAMPAIGN COUNTY, ILL. 333 U. S. 203, 92 L ed 649, 68 S. Ct. 461, (1948).

DOREMUS v. BOARD OF EDUCATION OF BOROUGH OF HAWTHORNE. 342 U. S. 429, 96 L ed 475, 72 S. Ct. 394, (1952).

ZORACH v. CLAUSON. 343 U. S. 306, 96 L ed 954, 72 S. Ct. 679, (1952).

ENGEL v. VITALE. 370 U. S. 421, 8 L ed 2d 601, 82 S. Ct. 1261, (1962).

SCHOOL DISTRICT OF ABINGTON TOWNSHIP, PENNSYLVANIA v. SCHEMPP.
MURRAY v. CURLETT.
374 U. S. 203, 10 L ed 2d 844, 83 S. Ct. 1560, (1963).

CHAMBERLIN v. DADE COUNTY, BOARD OF PUBLIC INSTRUCTION. 377 U. S. 402, 12 L ed 2d 407, 84 S. Ct. 1272, (1964).

EPPERSON v. ARKANSAS. 393 U. S. 97, 21 L Ed 2d 228, 89 S. Ct. 266, (1968).

WISCONSIN v. YODER. 406 U. S. 205, 32 L Ed 2d 15, 92 S. Ct. 1526, (1972).

The State and Sectarian Education

PIERCE v. SOCIETY OF THE SISTERS OF THE HOLY NAMES OF JESUS AND MARY.
PIERCE v. HILL MILITARY ACADEMY.
268 U. S. 510, 69 L. ed. 1070, 45 S. Ct. 571, (1925).

COCHRAN v. LOUISIANA STATE BOARD OF EDUCATION. 281 U. S. 370, 74 L. ed. 913, 50 S. Ct. 335, (1930).

EVERSON v. BOARD OF EDUCATION OF EWING TP 330 U. S. 1, 91 L ed 711, 67 S. Ct. 504, (1947).

BOARD OF EDUCATION OF CENTRAL SCHOOL DISTRICT NO. 1 v. ALLEN. 392 U. S. 236, 20 L Ed 2d 1060, 88 S. Ct. 1923, (1968).

FLAST v. COHEN. 392 U. S. 83, 20 L Ed 2d 947, 88 S. Ct. 1942, (1968).

TILTON v. RICHARDSON. 403 U. S. 672, 29 L Ed 2d 790, 91 S. Ct. 2091, (1971).

LEMON v. KURTZMAN.

    EARLEY v. DiCENSO.

    ROBINSON v. DiCENSO.

    403 U. S. 602, 29 L Ed 2d 745, 91 S. Ct. 2105, (1971).

LEMON v. KURTZMAN. 411 U. S. 192, 36 L Ed 2d 151, 93 S. Ct. 1463, (1973).

LEVITT v. COMMITTEE FOR PUBLIC EDUCATION AND RELIGIOUS LIBERTY.

    ANDERSON v. COMMITTEE FOR PUBLIC EDUCATION AND RELIGIOUS LIBERTY.

    CATHEDRAL ACADEMY v. COMMITTEE FOR PUBLIC EDUCATION AND RELIGIOUS LIBERTY.

    413 U. S. 472, 37 L Ed 2d 736, 93 S. Ct. 2814, (1973).

HUNT v. McNAIR. 413 U. S. 734, 37 L Ed 2d 923, 93 S. Ct. 2868, (1973).

COMMITTEE FOR PUBLIC EDUCATION AND RELIGIOUS LIBERTY v. NYQUIST.

    ANDERSON v. COMMITTEE FOR PUBLIC EDUCATION AND RELIGIOUS LIBERTY.

    NYQUIST v. COMMITTEE FOR PUBLIC EDUCATION AND RELIGIOUS LIBERTY.

    CHERRY v. COMMITTEE FOR PUBLIC EDUCATION AND RELIGIOUS LIBERTY.

    413 U. S. 756, 37 L Ed 2d 948, 93 S. Ct. 2955, (1973).

SLOAN v. LEMON.

    CROUTER v. LEMON.

    413 U. S. 825, 37 L Ed 2d 939, 93 S. Ct. 2982, (1973).

WHEELER v. BARRERA. 417 U. S. 402, 41 L Ed 2d 159, 94 S. Ct. 2274, (1974).

MEEK v. PITTINGER. 421 U. S. 349, 44 L Ed 2d 217, 95 S. Ct. 1753, (1975).

ROEMER v. BOARD OF PUBLIC WORKS OF MARYLAND. 426 U. S. 736, 49 L Ed 2d 179, 96 S. Ct. 2337, (1976).

WOLMAN v. WALTER. 433 U. S. 229, 53 L Ed 2d 714, 97 S. Ct. 2593, (1977).

APPENDIX B

The major decisions of the Supreme Court in the areas of religion-state controversy, excluding religion in public education and state aid to sectarian education, announced in the twenty-five years from the October Term, 1950, to the October Term, 1975, are listed in this Appendix with citation numbers from the *United States Reports*, the *United States Supreme Court Reports, Lawyers' Edition*, and the *Supreme Court Reporter*.

Religion and Taxation

FIRST UNITARIAN CHURCH OF LOS ANGELES v. COUNTY OF LOS ANGELES, CALIFORNIA.

VALLEY UNITARIAN-UNIVERSALIST CHURCH v. COUNTY OF LOS ANGELES, CALIFORNIA.

357 U. S. 545, 2 L Ed 2d 1484, 78 S. Ct. 1350, (1958).

WALZ v. TAX COMMISSION OF the CITY OF NEW YORK. 397 U. S. 664, 25 L ed 2d 697, 90 S. Ct. 1409, (1970).

DIFFENDERFER v. CENTRAL BAPTIST CHURCH OF MIAMI, FLORIDA, INC. 404 U. S. 412, 30 L ed 2d 567, 92 S. Ct. 574, (1972).

UNITED STATES v. CHRISTIAN ECHOES NATIONAL MINISTRY, INC. 404 U. S. 561, 30 L Ed 2d 716, 92 S. Ct. 663, (1972).

UNITED STATES v. AMERICAN FRIENDS SERVICE COMMITTEE. 419 U. S. 7, 42 L Ed 2d 7, 95 S. Ct. 13, (1974).

Sunday Observance

McGOWAN v. STATE OF MARYLAND. 366 U. S. 420, 6 L ed 2d 393, 81 S. Ct. 1101, (1961).

TWO GUYS FROM HARRISON-ALLENTOWN, INC. v. McGINLEY. 366 U. S. 582, 6 L ed 2d 551, 81 S. Ct. 1135, (1961).

BRAUNFELD v. BROWN. 366 U. S. 599, 6 L ed 2d 563, 81 S. Ct. 1144, (1961).

GALLAGHER v. CROWN KOSHER SUPER MARKET OF MASSACHUSETTS, INC. 366 U. S. 617, 6 L ed 2d 536, 81 S. Ct. 1122, (1961).

ARLAN'S DEPARTMENT STORE OF LOUISVILLE, INC. v. KENTUCKY. 371 U. S. 218, 9 L ed 2d 264, 83 S. Ct. 277, (1962).

Religious Freedom

NIEMOTKO v. STATE OF MARYLAND.

　KELLEY v. STATE OF MARYLAND.

　　340 U. S. 268, 95 L ed 267, 71 S. Ct. 325, (1951).

KUNZ v. PEOPLE OF STATE OF NEW YORK, 340 U. S. 290, 95 L ed 280, 71 S. Ct. 312, (1951).

FOWLER v. STATE OF RHODE ISLAND, 345 U. S. 67, 97 L ed 828, 73 S. Ct. 526, (1953).

POULOS v. STATE OF NEW HAMPSHIRE. 345 U. S. 395, 97 L ed 1105, 73 S. Ct. 760, (1953).

TORCASO v. WATKINS. 367 U. S. 488, 6 L ed 2d 982, 81 S. Ct. 1680, (1961).

SHERBERT v. VERNER. 374 U. S. 398, 10 L ed 2d 965, 83 S. Ct. 1790, (1963).

CRUZ v. BETO. 405 U. S. 319, 31 L Ed 2d 263, 92 S. Ct. 1079, (1972).

Church Governance

KEDROFF v. ST. NICHOLAS CATHEDRAL OF RUSSIAN ORTHODOX CHURCH IN NORTH AMERICA. 344 U. S. 94, 97 L ed 120, 73 S. Ct. 143, (1952).

KRESHIK v. SAINT NICHOLAS CATHEDRAL. 363 U. S. 190, 4 L ed 2d 1140, 80 S. Ct. 1037, (1960).

PRESBYTERIAN CHURCH IN the UNITED STATES v. MARY ELIZABETH BLUE HULL MEMORIAL PRESBYTERIAN CHURCH. 393 U. S. 440, 21 L Ed 2d 658, 89 S. Ct. 601, (1969).

MARYLAND AND VIRGINIA ELDERSHIP OF the CHURCHES OF GOD v. The CHURCH OF GOD AT SHARPSBURG, INC. 396 U. S. 367, 24 L Ed 2d 582, 90 S. Ct. 499, (1970).

SERBIAN EASTERN ORTHODOX DIOCESE FOR the UNITED STATES OF AMERICA AND CANADA v. MILIVOJEVICH. 426 U. S. 696, 49 L Ed 2d 151, 96 S. Ct. 2372, (1976).

Religion and Military Service

UNITED STATES v. NUGENT.

　UNITED STATES v. PACKER.

　　346 U. S. 1, 97 L ed 1417, 73 S. Ct. 991, (1953).

DICKINSON v. UNITED STATES. 346 U. S. 389, 98 L ed 132, 74 S. Ct. 152, (1953).

WITMER v. UNITED STATES. 348 U. S. 375, 99 L ed 428, 75 S. Ct. 392, (1955).